The Pharma Sales Success Formula: Shortcuts to Landing a Six Figure Job and Outselling Your Peers

by Scott M. Ellerbeck

ISBN: 1502399962
ISBN 13: 9781502399960

CONTENTS

Introduction

First, I would like to congratulate you on your decision to pursue a career in pharmaceuticals. Over the years I have found it to be a very exciting, rewarding, and lucrative career. Success can be found in every corner and behind every door.

Over the years this industry has also proven to be very stable. With new developments in biotechnology and genetic engineering coming along almost daily, this career has the potential to keep you well ahead of the pack for years into the future.

Why a Career in Pharmaceutical Sales Is So Desirable

The pharmaceutical industry is known for producing some of the best salespeople around. People who cut their teeth in pharmaceutical sales generally find it easy to transition into other sales jobs.

The pharmaceutical industry is a multibillion-dollar industry that helps people live better and more fulfilling lives every day. From new cancer therapies like PD1s (a new potential medication for melanoma, lung cancer, and many other cancers which may offer patients a new chance at life) to Nasonex (a nasal steroid that helps allergy sufferers get the most out of spring and summer), every moment of every day someone is being saved or helped by a pharmaceutical product or medical device. By choosing pharmaceutical sales as a career, you are going to play an integral role in this industry.

Personally, I love sales. In sales, you are moulding minds - you are convincing one person or business to think the way another person or business thinks. In the case of pharmaceuticals, you are changing medical practices and impacting peoples' lives with every call or contact you make.

The Rewards of a Career in Pharmaceutical Sales

This career has enabled me to raise a family very comfortably. I have a great house in a desirable neighborhood and have been able to travel the world, both through the business (which is nice because I don't pay a cent!) and on my own time, which is relaxing and mind-enriching.

There is a lot of variety within the career, which keeps it interesting year after year. A job in sales also offers a surprising and comforting degree of stability, as salespeople are usually the last to go in any organization because they are the key to growth.

A job in the pharmaceutical industry can be richly rewarding, not only with a nice salary and good bonuses but also with interesting and rewarding work. There are few things more satisfying than sitting in front of a doctor who responds positively to your product and knowing that a patient's life will be positively impacted because of the job you are doing.

The Role of Pharmaceuticals in the Medical World

Healthcare is a contentious business populated with many intelligent people, and most of those people are all too aware of the costs involved in caring for patients. Doctors alone are paid hundreds of thousands, or in some cases millions, of dollars a year.

Pharmaceuticals take up a very small fraction of the overall health care budget. In many cases new drugs will come onto the market which decrease costs, as decreased dosing and side effect profiles lead to less hospitalization time. Better drugs can also reduce doctors' reliance on pharmacists, because patients may require less support medication. This has effects all the way down the chain, from the doctor who treats the patient (and of course bills for the time they see the patient) to the nurses who look after the patient while in a hospital bed for their illness.

When we look at the scope of what pharmaceuticals do in this world we cannot help but be impressed. Since the dawn of humanity people have been picking herbs that have benefits to the human body, for example people ate the Foxglove plant (Digitalis purpurea) to drop blood pressure. This evolved into extractions from these plants to be used as proper pure medicines. Entering into this profession you can help take part in moving the health care system to adopt and bring in new and important innovations to save lives.

The Seven Rules of Sales

Throughout this book I will refer to these seven key rules of sales. I have gathered them over the years, and I will say without hesitation that they have given me the power to get to where I am in my pharmaceutical sales career.

Memorize these rules - they are like gold!

THE SEVEN RULES OF SALES

RULE #1: ASK AND YOU SHALL RECEIVE.

People need to do this more often. Ask for a hug from a loved one right now and I am sure you will get it. The same rule applies to sales: if you want to make a sale, you need to ask for it!

RULE #2: TWO EARS, ONE MOUTH.

Listen more. This is a hard trait to master as we all feel we need to speak to change the world. Try listening to others' problems and then answering only when they have finished speaking.

RULE #3: WHOEVER SPEAKS FIRST LOSES.

Once you give the grand finale and ask to close the sale, be quiet and wait. The uncomfortable silence can easily be broken with an agreement to buy your idea.

RULE #4: THE 80/20 RULE.

Eighty percent of your business will come from twenty percent of your clients. Focus the maximum effort on that twenty percent.

RULE #5: THE BEST WAY TO SELL TO HAVE SOMEONE SELL FOR YOU.

In your own life, how many times has your spouse, best friend, or someone else you love and trust convinced you to buy something?

RULE #6: DO NOT PREACH IN THE DESERT.

Find out who your customers are and stick to them like glue. Rarely will I talk business with friends. First, they are not interested; second, it is a poor way to make money.

RULE #7: ONE SALE GIVES YOU THREE OTHERS.

Rules number five and seven go hand in hand. One buyer, once fully convinced, will tell all their friends about their great buy and will try to convince those friends to seek out the same bargain they found.

SECTION ONE:
GETTING INTO THE BUSINESS

Chapter 1: Finding Contacts

What You'll Learn in This Chapter:

1. Why you need to market YOURSELF first.

2. How to start your pharmaceutical industry contact list.

3. How to contact North America's top ten pharmaceutical companies.

4. Tips for growing your contact list.

5. Little-used sources of "insider" industry contact information.

Over the years, many people have commented to me that the pharmaceutical industry is very difficult to get into. But the fact is, if you follow some very easy steps you will be hired in no time.

I'm sure you've heard the statement "You need to treat getting a job like it is a job." Well, it's true. You are selling a product, much like you soon will be selling pharmaceuticals. In this case, the most expensive and valuable product is you!

For this reason, the first section of this book is devoted to teaching you how best to market and sell yourself.

Key Concept:
When you're getting started in sales, YOU are the product!

If you are going to sell a product, you'll have to figure out who is going to buy it. The buyers, or potential buyers, will be referred to as "contacts" in this book from now on. So get out a piece of paper - it's time to make a list of the contacts you may have within the pharmaceutical industry.

Getting Started with a Contact List

My contact list is my livelihood. If I were to lose my job tomorrow I would get out my Rolodex, Outlook contacts folder, Gmail contacts folder, and Linked In account and have a look through and see who I really know.

I rarely discard business cards and have been on the road for fifteen years, so I have close to 2500 contacts. In my list of people is someone who either has a job for me or has a lead to get me a job with someone else.

LinkedIn has become an easy and convenient way to keep track of your business contacts and grow your network. I would highly recommend joining and making an account. Using the company search features, it is easy to see who is linked to whom. This can allow you to get introduced to so many new people in your targeted industry. People in the pharmaceutical industry are highly active on LinkedIn, so this is a fantastic way to get connected.

Let's get back to the piece of paper. Start creating a contact list for yourself. Write it out in this format:

Name	Company	Position	Phone and Email	Last Call	Notes
Ace Heart	Pfizer	Sales Rep	234-2343 ace.heart@pfizer.com	Mar 17, 14	
Nels Steroid	Merck	Specialist Rep	876-4657 nels.steroid@merck.com	Mar 17, 14	
Tam O'Fine	Sanofi	Manager	987-1234 tam.ofine@sanofi.com	Mar 17, 14	

This format is pretty straightforward. You need the following information:

- A **name**, of course.
- The **company** that this contact works for.
- The **position** held by the contact (Representative, Specialist Representative, Manager, etc.).
- The contact's **phone number**.
- The **last date** you contacted them.
- Progress **notes** for any other important information.

As you will learn later in this chapter, the name of the company each contact works for will become important later as you build yourself a company power structure map.

Here's a special trick: you can sometimes guess what the person's email address is by following the simple formula firstname.lastname@companyname.com. If you look at the boxes above you can see some examples of real companies with made up employees.

Adding New Contacts to Your List

Before you start worrying that you have already contacted all the friends you know in the industry and it has got you nowhere, keep reading for some tricks to find new contacts within the industry.

If you really don't know anyone in the industry, fine – there are other ways of finding contacts. First, compile a list of pharmaceutical companies that you know, along with contact information and the location and phone number of their head office.

For your convenience, here are the top ten:

Company	Phone or Web contact (USA)	Phone (Canada)
Johnson & Johnson	1-732-524-0400	1-877-223-9807
Pfizer	1-212-733-2323	1-514-693-4623 or 1-877-633-2001
Roche Pharmaceuticals	1-973-235-5000 http://careers.roche.com/en/contact_form.html	1-800-561-1759
Glaxo Smith Kline	1-888-825-5249	1-905-819-3000
Novartis	1-888-669-6682	1-514-631-6775
Sanofi	1-800-981-2491	1-514-331-9220 or 1-800-363-6364
Astrazeneca	1-302-886-3000 or 1-800-456-3669	1-905-277-7111 or 1-800-668-6000
Abbott Laboratories	1-212-546-4000	1-800-267-1088
Merck	1-908-423-1000	1-514-428-8600 or 1-800-567-2594
Bayer	1-412-777-2000	1-416-248-0771

More Strategies for Finding New Contacts

For other companies you can usually get the phone number from their web site. You can also use the internet to find out if they have any regional offices that are close to you. Regional offices are great because they have a lot of information that is specific to your local area. By dropping in, you can usually meet up with an area manager.

You may also decide to get the corporate address for a company's human resources department and send in a resume.

Unless you already have a very impressive resume, a mass mailing of your resume with a "To Whom It May Concern" cover letter is not going to do much good. This strategy may be worth a shot for the sake of covering all bases, but most organizations are run by a few decision-makers (the rest of the employees fill supporting roles) and a mass mailing of your resume simply will not get your name in front of the true decision-makers.

Insider Tip:
Most "mass mailed" resumes are filed under "G" for "Garbage!"

Virtually all companies these days require you to apply for positions online. You go to the company website, find a job posting, fill in the template, and attach your resume. This strategy is never going to hurt you and I think it should always be done as a starting point, but just like a mass mailing of your resume, I would not rely on this as a good way to get a job.

When I was hiring people for sales positions, these computer based resume programs would sometimes give me hundreds of resumes. If the human resources department was understaffed, which it often is, I would not even have them pre-screened. The point is that you don't want to be caught up in the masses - you want to stand out from the crowd. The best way to do this is to have an inside track on the people that make up the company.

In the next chapter, we will take a look at far more effective strategies you can use to get in deeper and find the decision-makers.

Now, let's look at how you can actually begin contacting the real people behind the big corporate image; these are the people who really make the company what it is.

Grow Your Contact List by Talking with Doctors

One excellent trick for finding new contacts is to visit your personal physician. Tell them and their office assistant of your plans to enter the industry, and ask to look through their list of contacts in the pharmaceutical industry.

Most medical clinics will have a *huge* list of company cards that you can look through. Go through them and write down names and phone numbers. A medical clinic's contact list is a great resource, as it is most likely up to date and will list pharmaceutical salespeople who are currently making daily visits to sell their products.

If your doctor is a "core" physician (more on this in a minute), this little trick of asking your doctor for business cards will most likely net you the names and contact numbers of every major pharmaceutical salesperson in your area!

Insider Tip:
A "Core" or "Key" physician is a doctor who prescribes a lot of pharmaceuticals, usually because they are a good doctor and are therefore very busy.

Core physicians can be general practitioners or specialists, and may have useful contacts for many different product types or just one. For example, a cardiologist (heart specialist) will prescribe a lot of heart medication, but little to no chemotherapies.

Sometimes there will be medical conventions in your town. As an outsider you can often register for these conventions for a small fee. Usually you will find a number of companies have set up booths to attract physicians during the breaks and at lunch, so a lot of the time the sales reps that are working the booths while the convention is on have plenty of time to talk. This gives you a chance to introduce yourself to a number of key companies and the people that work at the sales booths. This is an excellent way to get some quality time with people in a work setting with a lot of down time.

Grow your Contacts List by Talking with Pharmacists

Pharmacists, like physicians, can be a wealth of information on the pharmaceutical industry. All one has to do is to go into any pharmacy and start looking not at the products themselves, but at who the manufacturers are.

You will find dozens of companies, many of whom you have never even heard of before. One reason for this is that a company's name will remain the same even if it was acquired by a larger company. For example if you look on the back of a box of an antihistamine called Claritin, you will find the company name Schering. This company was bought by Merck, but the name still stays on the products.

Pharmacists can give you the names of the companies and company representatives that they deal with. This should be a wealth of current information. The best sales reps have very close ties to the pharmacies as they understand the value of these shops for information.

One of my old mentors in the industry feels that the "hospital" pharmacist is the key to many of the connections. He has a good point - all the major companies are operating in hospitals and they truly are the hub of the medical community.

Now you have learned a couple of tricks for obtaining names within the pharmaceutical industry so that you can start putting faces behind the corporate logos. By using your current contacts (friends, colleagues, your physician, etc.), you will be able to leverage and increase the number of people who you know in the industry.

In the next chapter, you'll learn insider strategies for managing your contact list to keep it growing.

Online Resources to Help You Grow Your Contacts

The availability of websites like LinkedIn has added a whole new dimension to the world of networking. LinkedIn is an essential tool for any business professional today. This site did not even exist 12 years ago and has done nothing but grow in importance since coming online. Ensure that your resume is on LinkedIn at the very least. I have never done this personally, but many people I have worked with are writing articles and posting them to this site on a regular basis.

In Canada have a look at this website:

http://www.stacommunications.com/journals/cpm/

It offers many different articles to read about the pharmaceutical industry and has a many back issues you can go through. Try contacting some of the authors, as they may be willing to help you in your search. Remember Rule Number One: ask and you shall receive.

Another great website for all sorts of information on the pharmaceutical industry is www.cafepharma.com. This is more dedicated to the United States marketplace, but there is so much to this site that everyone should have a look at it. This is an anonymous chat room in many cases and the comments go from intelligent and informative to abusive, so take some of it with a grain of salt.

Key Strategies from This Chapter:

1. When you're getting started in sales, remember that the **first product you need to market is YOU.**

2. **Create a pharmaceutical industry contact list.** For each contact record their name, company, job title, phone number, and the last date you contacted them.

   You should also include progress notes for each contact to remind yourself what happened during your last contact with them and how and when to follow up with them.

3. **Grow your contact list** by searching your phone book and the internet for people and companies in your industry.

4. Your personal physician is a great source of pharmaceutical industry contacts.

Chapter 2:
Managing Your Contacts

What You'll Learn in This Chapter:

1. Strategies for getting your doctor to share top contacts.

2. The secret trick head-hunters use to add new contacts to their lists.

More Strategies for Getting Contacts from Your Doctor

So how does your contact list look? Right now - or at least by the time you finish reading this chapter - it should look something like this:

BIG PHARMA NUMBER 1

Representatives	Phone #
1. John Depot	578-8768
2. Ace Inhibit	987-2348
3. Cort Ico	345-3456
4. Trey Cycle	345-9999

District Manager for Above	Phone #
Penny Cyllin	233-9898

So how do you create this list? Let's say, for example, that you went to speak with your doctor and told them of your desire to work in the pharmaceutical industry. Do they know anyone who works in the industry? Do they have any people whom they enjoy meeting with?

"Yes," they reply, "there are so many drugs out there that it is hard to keep track of them. However, there is this guy, Cort Ico, who really helped me out the other day with a patient of mine who has terrible psoriasis."

Your doctor suggested that you call Cort, as he is friendly and approachable. Now you are making some good progress - but you don't stop there. You then ask, "Hey, would you mind if I browse through your medical cards and get some names of other people in the industry?" Boom! You hit a jackpot! If your doctor is a core doctor, they will have many cards and contacts. From this doctor alone, you might get fifty names.

Rule to Remember:
The first rule of sales is "Ask and you shall receive".

As another bonus, you also manage to get three names of some district managers who sometimes go around with the representatives for a ride-along or a work-with and have left their cards with the doctor as well.

So now your list looks like this:

BIG PHARMA NUMBER 1

Representatives	Phone #
1. John Depot	578-8768
2. Ace Inhibit	987-2348
3. Cort Ico	345-3456
4. Trey Cycle	345-9999

District Manager for Above	Phone #
Penny Cyllin	233-9898

BIG PHARMA NUMBER 2

Representatives	Phone #
1. Ace Heart	249-6845
2. Cort Steroid	687-5289
3. Tax O'Fin	654-2562

District Manager for Above	Phone #
Zoe Loft	232-2541

Continue filling out this list with all the other companies that you are aware of.

Your Company Power Structure Map

As you build your contact list, you are ultimately trying to create a power structure map or "family tree" of the corporation. For example:

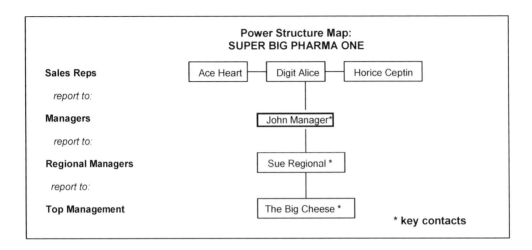

The important thing to remember about this power structure is that it is up to the key contacts (starred) to do the hiring. The fourth rule of sales states that 80 percent of your business comes from 20 percent of your contacts. These are your **core contacts** - the people who will give you the job.

A Head-hunter's Trick for Finding New Contacts

If you are missing some company names, there is another trick you can use to get them added to your contact list. A head-hunter taught me this one when I inquired where she had got my name. (Later in this book, I will talk more about head-hunters and why they can be a great resource for you.)

The technique is this: call up the regional office or main head office and ask the person who answers the phone for the name of the representative for the region that you would like to cover as a territory.

Now, you can't just call and ask, "Who is your sales rep for Alberta?" (or Iowa, or California...) because a company may have hundreds of people working in one region. Try to be as specific as possible. I would use the name of a medical office that is near your house or in your vicinity.

Key Secret:
*When inquiring about the sales reps for a region,
be specific – use the name of a local medical office.*

An example would be phoning the Roche Pharmaceuticals head office in Canada and asking, "Could I get the name of the salesperson in charge of, or calling on, Sunny Stone Medical Center at 126 Meadow Street, Los Angeles, California?"

Much of the time, the person answering will give you the District Manager (or "DM") as the contact for the whole region just by default. This is a bonus, as it is the DM who is doing the hiring for the most part, but you do want the names of individual salespeople as well. They are a great source of information about the DM when your interview comes up.

This little trick is how my head-hunter friend gets names of salespeople, and especially specialist sales representatives. When she asks, she specifies a particular hospital and drug. For example, she might call the Roche Pharmaceuticals head office in Canada and ask, "Could I have the name of the salesperson in charge of Rituximab at the Sunnybrook Hospital in Toronto?"

You can start doing this right away with the top pharmaceutical companies listed earlier in Chapter One. The names of each company's most important focus drugs are easy to find on their web sites.

Once you are working in sales, this one of the exact techniques you will use to find doctors in your territory who see patients within your disease group. For example, I find pathologists to be a wealth of information. They truly are the heart of a hospital. In cancer treatments, if anything gets cut out the pathologists are the ones who analyze it. They can tell you who is doing the cutting and where the patients are going. Quite simply, they can keep providing you with more and more contacts.

By now you are starting to get quite a few names. What are you going to do with them?

Key Strategies from This Chapter:

1. **Ask and you shall receive!** Ask your doctor for their favorite contacts, then follow up by asking if you can go through their own contact list.

2. **One contact gets you three more.** Any time you make one new contact in this field, they can easily become a source of three additional contacts – or sometimes many more!

3. To fill out your contact list for a region, call regional or head offices and ask who their sales reps are in your area.

   Remember to be specific – for the best results, use the name of a local medical office. It's also a good idea to ask for the local rep responsible for a single drug or product.

Chapter 3:
Maximizing Your Contacts

What You'll Learn in This Chapter:

1. A key strategy for maximizing the value of every contact you talk with.

2. The one key area where most people fail when starting out in pharmaceutical sales.

3. Why it's crucial to develop lasting relationships with your contacts.

Talking with your new contacts is the fun part of this whole process. You get to meet and converse with a number of new and exciting people, some of whom may become your future colleagues.

So pick up the phone!

Or if you're not in too much of a hurry, hold on and read a little more. I will try to give you a few ideas to help you steer the conversation with your new contacts, and arm you with more knowledge so that you can carry on an intelligent conversation.

How to Maximize the Value of Every Contact You Talk With

Sales reps calling on general practitioners are usually pretty chatty and would like nothing more than to talk doctors' ears off about what they do every day. This brings us to another rule of sales:

Rule to Remember:
The second rule of sales is "Two Ears, One Mouth (listen, listen, listen!)"

Have you ever had a conversation with someone who talked your ear off? I don't know about you, but unless it is my mother or my best friend, I find this quite annoying. (And even with your mother or best friend, it can get to be a bit much.)

On the other hand, if the roles are reversed and someone is really listening to you and asking you intelligent questions that are pertinent to the conversation… well, everyone loves that!

In the past, I have walked into an interview and had the client telling me all about their business within minutes of starting the interview. They will then talk for an hour with me, during which time I can learn a lot about their challenges and weaknesses.

Of course I will ask a few leading questions, but for the most part they do the talking. This is, after all, what they do every day. It is their passion, so speaking about it puts them at peace and relaxes them. After all, who doesn't enjoy talking about themselves?

This is *exactly* what your goal is when talking with your new contact within the industry. You want them to tell you everything you can learn about entering the industry, particularly within their company's particular business realm. Don't worry about telling them about yourself; this will come. By just listening, you are telling them about a huge strength you possess – your listening skills.

Most companies are very specific as to the type of treatment they specialize in. For example, Merck is a cardiovascular specialty company. Roche is a powerhouse in the treatment of cancer.

You should also get to know the company politics and culture. How much of a process-driven company is it? How much paperwork is associated with the company? When you talk with most salespeople they will tell you that they have piles of paperwork, but you need to find out what this actually means. How many calls will you be required to make per day? How many notes are required per call?

These types of questions will give you a good idea of what is required. You might even ask a contact to show you what they mean when they talk about their company's requirements - this will really show your interest.

Meeting for coffee is an excellent way to accomplish all of the above. When you are speaking over the phone with a new contact, make a habit of finishing the conversation with. "Thanks so much for your time - I learned a lot and would love to meet you for coffee to discuss more."

Do not worry about people not wanting to entertain your questions. If I have learned one thing, it is that people love to talk about themselves and their business.

ALWAYS Follow Up

Since starting in this industry, I have been approached by a huge number of people about getting into pharmaceuticals. I have always told them the same thing: "Call me anytime to ask questions. Send me your resume." I remind them about not forgetting to call, and that I need reminding myself.

This really is a weeding-out process. Research shows that physicians need to hear the name of a new drug *five* times before they remember it. I believe that this also holds true if you are trying to get your name out as someone who wants into the business.

What does this mean? It means you need to make at *least* five calls per contact.

Key Secret:
Physicians need to hear the name of a new drug FIVE TIMES
before they remember it!

Guess what? The vast majority of the people who contact me never even send a resume. Of the ones who do send a resume, only a few follow up with phone calls.

So here we have someone wanting to get into an industry with unlimited growth potential and the potential to make six figures - heck, even seven or eight figures if you move into upper management. These people don't even follow up with someone who offers to talk with them anytime and share further information about the industry that they would like to enter.

The Importance of Maintaining Ongoing Contact

Each meeting with every contact on your list must be treated like a sales call.

When I first walk into a physician's office, it's pretty unlikely that the doctor will say, "Thank God you showed up! The next fifty patients will be going on your drug!" The amount of information a doctor needs to safely use your product is immense. "Do no harm" is the motto of the physician's world. The amount of information the physician will need to safely administer your product is great, and selling will therefore take time.

You cannot rush the process of making a sale in the medical world. This is especially true of higher-end drugs like new oncology products or biotechnology, but it really is the case with all products. You must not forget that you are dealing with medicine - and any medicine, if not used properly, carries a risk of death.

This is why it is vital for you to establish and maintain ongoing contact with everyone on your list. People in the pharmaceutical business are like everyone else; we all get together and chat. If there are no job openings in my company, I can guarantee that I know many other salespeople at other companies that just might be looking for someone new.

Whenever possible, get names and plan another follow-up meeting. I enjoy coffee because for me one of life's joys is meeting new people and learning new things.

These meetings, even if they are casual, are actually your first job interviews.

Key Strategies from This Chapter:

1. **The best way to get key information from a contact is to listen.** Open a conversation and encourage them to talk about themselves and their work. Remember: two ears, one mouth!

2. **Always follow up with contacts.** Most doctors need to hear the name of a new product five times before they remember it – you can't expect to form a lasting impression in anyone's mind without a few repeat calls. Follow up often and build lasting relationships.

Chapter 4:
Interviewing

What You'll Learn in This Chapter:

1. The best way to open an interview with a contact.

2. How to maximize the value of your previous accomplishments – even if you have no pharmaceutical sales experience.

3. The one critical action you *must* take when ending an interview.

When I say that you should meet people for coffee, make no mistake: this is an interview!

By now, you have learned enough concepts and strategies not only to *increase* the number of contacts on your list, but also to *manage* these contacts to bring you more contacts, including some district managers.

You have convinced a few physicians to share their contact lists with you. You have opened conversations with these people, listened, and followed up with them to start building relationships. And through your growing web of contacts, you have arranged to meet with one or more district managers.

Even though they may not have any positions open, one may open in the next day or two. A district manager may also know of other companies who are hiring. So when you meet with them, remember that this is not just a cup of coffee – it's a job interview.

Starting an Interview

I will not pretend to be an expert on the interview process. However, what I can offer you is a number of excellent techniques that have worked many times for me and my colleagues.

First, remember that even an "informational interview" is a sales pitch. You are selling yourself!

Ensure that you read Section Three of this book to sharpen your selling skills before proceeding with an interview. Regardless of whom you are seeing - a representative, specialist, district manager, director of a division, or even a company president - your interview will be far more likely to land you a job if you follow the basic principles of selling that are laid out in Section Three.

In any interview, you should follow these four steps:

1. **Start with an opening** to get your interviewer talking.

2. **Probe for information** about the type of person they are looking for, and listen carefully to their response.

3. **Tell them about how you match the profile** they have given you and how your skills fit with what they need.

4. **Get a commitment** that they would like to have you working for them.

Interviews are an ever-changing process. If you have trouble with interviews, I encourage you to read more about them in other general interview books. Generally, the key to a pleasant and effective interview is to relax and carry on a conversation with the person about their business.

Linking Your Skills to Your Accomplishments

A common style of interview is the "interactive" interview, in which the interviewer (the person you are meeting with) asks the interviewee (you) a question, then asks related questions to get you to elaborate further on your answer and link it to related experience you may have.

The process is very simple and goes something like this:

Interviewer:

"What are your greatest skills that you believe would help you succeed in this position?"

Interviewee:

"I have strong selling skills, great interpersonal relations, and a strong drive to succeed."

Interviewer:

"Can you give me an example from the last three months of how you have used your creative selling skills (interpersonal relations, etc.)?"

The process here is that the interviewer asks questions that require you to link a skill you have to a recent accomplishment. From that one skill that you give the interviewer may ask a number of questions designed to dig deeper and deeper into your skill set.

Key Strategy:
When interviewing, link the skills
you are discussing to past accomplishments.

It is the small details that are going to help you land the job. Imagine that the interviewer is asking you to tell a story with every question. The better and more interesting the story is, the more the interviewer is going to enjoy the interview.

Think of it like someone asking you to tell them about catching a fish. They don't want to know what the map looked like. They want to hear that the salmon did a magical tail dance on the water and the spray sent rainbows up from the water. Sell the sizzle.

Focus not only on your actions, but also the results of your actions. For example, the interviewer may ask, "Tell me about a time when you had to deal with a difficult customer. What did you do to bring them around?" A question like this is designed to give you an opportunity to use real examples from your working past. Before your interviews you need to think of about four or five specific examples that you can use. Think about all the specific actions you have taken and details about the effects of your actions.

"What have you done in the past to improve your work performance?" "Can you describe some activities that you do to keep yourself organized?" Think your examples through in great detail and focus on actions that you have taken as well as the outcomes. Actions and outcomes are the key to ensuring you tell a story that the interviewer is going to like.

"Have you ever had to resolve a conflict with a co-worker? How did you resolve it? How about a conflict with a manager or boss?" These questions are great opportunities to show the interviewer how well you work with others. Again the way to answer these is to tell a story about your actions and the outcomes.

Everyone applying for the job thinks that they have special skills. Your interviewer knows this all too well, so they are trying to establish what type of skills you really have by getting you to give examples of how you have actually used each particular skill.

The key here is to be prepared. Make a list of your accomplishments that show what a talented salesperson you are, so you will have some concrete examples ready when you are in an interview. Try to come up with four or five examples per skill set. This will make it easier for you to relax in the interview.

Also, don't feel that you have to deliver an answer the second that the interviewer finishes asking a question. Take a minute to think about your answer if you need to.

Finally, don't limit yourself to using examples from previous work experience. If you have a better example from a volunteer position, a hobby or club, or even your personal life, use it. For example, in response to the question about being a creative person, you might talk about a creative way you solved a problem for a friend, relative, or neighbor. Just don't overdo this - for the most part you need to talk about your work experience.

How to Get Your Interviewer Talking

As an interviewee, I am always trying to get my interviewer to start talking. After answering an interviewer's question, I make a point of following up my answer with a quick question of my own.

A great question to ask is, "Out of curiosity, what traits do you think would be most valuable for someone working in this position?" The answer could very well give you the key to the interview!

And don't stop there - keep your interviewer talking. This not only shows that you are interested in the business and willing to listen, it also helps to ease some of the pressure of the "grilling" that comes with an interview. Remember that the interview is about you, but getting a healthy conversation going with the interviewer is going to help your cause (unless you really overdo it).

Overcoming the "No Experience" Objection

Another question you may be asked is "What problems or weaknesses do you have?" Without question, if I were starting out in the business today, I would answer "Lack of experience in the pharmaceutical industry." This is an objection that you *must* address before closing the interview and getting the job.

Interview Tip:
If you don't have pharmaceutical sales experience,
you must be ready to address this objection when it comes up.

The key to overcoming this objection is to respond with a question or statement such as one of the following:

- "Have you hired someone without pharmaceutical sales experience in the past?"

- "What was it about them that you liked? What traits did they have?"

- "Let me share a story that may alleviate your concern about my lack of previous pharmaceutical experience...

- "Before starting in pharmaceutical sales, I was a liquor salesperson. In this job I had to manage a number of contacts. True, they were bar and liquor store managers, not doctors, but this sales experience had many things in common with pharmaceutical sales that I can certainly transfer."

A pharmaceutical sales position is in "outside sales", meaning that you are selling to clients outside of an established shop, warehouse, or office building. You are a travelling salesperson visiting clients in their place of work. Your interviewer must feel comfortable taking the risk of hiring a person without experience in the industry.

To continue addressing this objection, show your interviewer why it makes more sense to take a risk hiring you than to hire some "old blood" with plenty of experience but lots of bad habits. Tell your interviewer, "I understand that you have concerns about hiring someone new to the industry. I know that I can never take away the risk associated with this, but I do have other experiences that are transferable."

It will help for you to get ready by writing out and rehearsing a detailed response to this objection for when it comes up.

Ending the Interview

Any interview with a potential employer must end with a *commitment.*

What kind of commitment should you be looking for? My personal favorite question, and one that is a personal standard, goes like this: *"Based on what we have discussed today, are you ready to offer me this position?"* This response usually raises some hackles when I tell people to use it, but let's go through some scenarios of what may happen.

The best response would be a resounding "YES!" Great! Break out the Dom Perignon - you have the job! As the first rule of sales states, "ask and you shall receive."

The second scenario is a "NO." Can you handle the rejection? I certainly hope so, because when you get a job in the pharmaceutical industry, lots of doctors are going to tell you "NO." Remember: the important thing is what you do with the NO after you hear it.

What is a "NO"? Those of you who have skipped ahead to Section Three on selling skills may recognize it as an *objection.* It needs to be handled.

Ask yourself this: would you rather not ask this simple question and walk out of the interview thinking that you had the job… and then wait for the call that may never come? I would not.

Whether you receive a YES or a NO, at least you now have something to deal with. If you have received a NO, you know that your interview technique has been unsuccessful, and that you need to make it right before you can get the job.

Key Strategy:
Always end an interview with a commitment
from the person you are meeting.

Ultimately, you will need to deal with your interviewer's objections, whatever those may be. The easiest way that I have found to do this is to ask the simple question, "What reservations do you currently have that I can attempt to address?"

Pay attention to your interviewer's response and at the very least you will come away from the interview with a clear idea of what objections you still need to address.

If your interviewer gives an answer like "We don't have any openings right now," you can always respond with a final question such as "Would it be all right if I contacted you in a few weeks to see if anything has changed?" or "If the situation did change, would you be willing to offer me the job?" This will help you gain the commitment even if there is no opening in the company at present.

Remember, a coffee meeting with a representative – even if they have no power to hire, or no knowledge of any openings – is an interview! These reps have the power to influence decision makers within a company where you may wish to be hired.

Key Strategies from This Chapter:

1. **When opening an interview, stay relaxed** and ask your interviewer lots of questions. Most people love to talk about themselves and their business, so this is a great opportunity for you to learn a lot about the industry. Ask and listen!

2. **Prepare your responses** for questions about your pharmaceutical sales experience. If you have none, make a list of your accomplishments that demonstrate you could make a good pharmaceutical sales rep.

3. **End every interview with a commitment** from the interviewer. Don't be afraid to ask for one! Remember the first rule of sales: Ask and you shall receive.

Chapter 5:
What to Wear

What You'll Learn in This Chapter:

1. Why dressing well helps your job prospects.

2. What to wear – men and women.

What to Wear – Men

Get yourself a business suit. Men's fashion has not changed very much since the 1800s, so rest assured that you can use a suit for a long time if it is of good quality.

Dark colors are much more acceptable than light colors. It is said that your first suit should be dark blue. I never wear non-matching pants and jacket; some people disagree with me on this, but I prefer to dress conservatively.

If you walk into an interview wearing a good quality blue suit, a nicely pressed shirt, and a tie your clothing will be a non-issue and your skills will be discussed. The last thing that you want your interviewer thinking is "What is with that lime-green jacket?" even if it is the rage and on the cover of GQ Magazine. Your new prospective manager may not have picked up that issue.

Key Point:
If they're thinking about your looks,
they're not thinking about your skills.

What to Wear – Women

The same goes for women. My most successful female colleagues dress conservatively in good quality business suits. A good suit is well worth the investment, as the return is potentially a six-figure income.

As for dressing provocatively, I won't lie - it works for some managers. Will it guarantee you a job? Really, I don't think that anything can, but I know of district managers who believe that physicians buy drugs based on a salesperson's looks. In my opinion, this is rarely the case.

The old saying is true: beauty is only skin deep. In sales, we are trying to build long-lasting relationships, and those relationships should be built on something more substantial than a sexy outfit.

Key Strategies from This Chapter:

1. If you dress **conservatively and with taste**, interviewers are left free to discuss your skills. If they're looking at your unusual outfit, they're not focusing on whether or not you're a good fit for the job.

2. **Avoid the temptation to wear sexy outfits**, even if that tactic has worked for you in the past. Remember that you are working to build long-lasting relationships, and dress accordingly.

Chapter 6:
A Ride-Along and a Head-hunter

What You'll Learn in This Chapter:

1. How a ride-along can get your foot in the door.

2. What head-hunters do and how they can help you.

3. Tips for dealing with head-hunters and negotiating salary.

I am putting these two categories together because when I was starting out in the industry, the first interview question any head-hunter would ask is, "Have you ever been on a ride-along?" When someone asks you this question, you want to be able to say "Yes!"

What Is a Ride-Along?

A ride-along is a "job shadow" exercise, and it is a great way to see if this job is for you. For one day or a few days, you tag along and make sales calls with some company representatives and see what happens.

On a ride-along, you'll watch different types of sales situations and the different interactions that you might go through as a representative with the company. This will give you some good ideas for your budding career, and it will also help you build a relationship with someone inside the industry.

A ride-along also could be the start of a mentorship program, which I would highly recommend. In Chapter 17 of this book, you will learn more about this type of program and how it can help jump-start your career.

What to Do During a Ride-Along

During the ride-along, make note of as many details as possible about the job you will be doing. What type of drugs are they selling? Who are they selling them to? These details could be important later in the interview process - especially if you happen to be interviewing with the company that you did the ride-along with.

Find out what the job entails. A ride-along gives you a good idea of what you will be doing on a day-to-day basis. Is this really a job that you would be interested in?

I would suggest going for a ride-along with as many people as will take you. When you are building your first contact list and making your initial phone calls with representatives in the industry, your first objective should be gaining a commitment for a ride-along. Going for a ride-along is an exercise that you will be able to mention later when asked if you have any experience in the industry.

What Is a Head-hunter and How Can They Help You?

A head-hunter is someone who finds and recruits professionals who would be suitable for a workforce. Head-hunters are useful resources within the pharmaceutical industry for a number of reasons. I see these people as the "agents" of our industry - they are dialed in and know much about what is happening within the industry.

It is important to find an employment agency that specializes in the pharmaceutical industry. There will usually be one or two of these in any large urban center. The best way to find them is simply to look up agencies in the yellow pages under "Employment Agencies," then phone each agency and ask what they specialize in. If they specialize in another industry, ask them for a referral to the agency that specializes in the pharmaceutical industry. Ensure that you contact any agencies that you are referred to.

That said, it is important to know a few things about the relationship you will have with head-hunters.

First, head-hunters make a living by placing professionals within the industry, for which they receive a commission based on a percentage of the salary of the people they place. This commission is paid by the company that ends up hiring the employee, so the job seeker does not pay anything directly to the head-hunter.

A district manager looking for new sales reps will usually approach one or two reputable employment firms that specialize in the industry. A head-hunter from each employment firm will then put forward the names of about eight people they feel would be suitable for the position. Because the head-hunter has screened these potential employees for their skills and aptitudes, the DM benefits by not having to screen 30 to 100 candidates before finding the right one.

When you are dealing with head-hunters, remember that they are running a business and that they are paid by the company doing the hiring. You are not their client - you are their product.

Employment agencies are usually limited in the number of names they can put forward to each client. When I was using head-hunters to hire I would often give them a limited number of people I would see. Most often I would only see a maximum of five candidates. This saved me time as I could be assured that the head-hunter would give me their five best candidates. If you don't have much pharmaceutical sales experience they may not put your name forward, but don't take this personally. Other candidates may have worked the region previously, or sold competitive products in the same class. This is much more of an issue these days as companies have been laying off people in very large numbers, so there are a lot of skilled people looking for work in the pharmaceutical industry.

Point to Remember:
When dealing with head-hunters, remember that you are
their product, not their client.

I have one colleague who used to trade favors with the head-hunters. My friend would offer a potential job - for example he might say, "Pfizer is hiring for Edmonton North." In exchange, the head-hunter would put my friend's name forward to some other job leads that he would have.

A few phone calls to contacts within the industry will tell you which placement firms specialize in pharmaceutical jobs. Once you are in the industry, the head-hunters who work at these firms will be valuable resources for a number of reasons. For one, they will let you know how competitive your salary is. I consider them almost like sports agents. When they approach you with new positions, there is always a salary attached. This is another reason I feel that pharmaceuticals is such a great industry - I have been approached with a number of very attractive offers from head-hunters!

Tips for Dealing with Head-hunters and Negotiating Salary

About six months ago, I was approached by one of my friends who is a head-hunter. He is the specialist for my area. The job was with a new biotechnology company, and it had a great product portfolio and a lot of potential. The salary was around $80,000 a year, with experience and bonus potential of $30,000.

I politely declined the offer and said I most likely could not consider it - or any job, for that matter - unless the base was $100,000. This is reasonable when you consider that I would be leaving the security of my current position to move to an unknown start-up company with new products. I would have to move to a head office somewhere for at least three weeks to learn about the new products. There is a lot of work associated with a company move - is it really worth it for a $5,000 raise, which means that after taxes I would be taking home an extra $125 with each paycheque?

My friend laughed and said that the company was 20 percent off the $100,000 mark and it might be a while till any company was willing to pay this level.

About three months later, the phone rang and he made me an offer of $100,000 base salary and $30,000 more in bonus. I am not telling you this to brag, but to give you some idea of the potential of the industry and how to stay on top of salaries through head-hunters. These people are always linked in to the industry and what is happening on the salary level. Keep them close - they are a great asset.

Key Strategy:
Before accepting an offer from a head-hunter,
consider the hidden costs and risks of taking a new job.

Head-hunters are also an excellent way for you to find out about major movements within the industry and new products that are coming out. They are usually one of the first to know of an expanding sales force, an increase in salaries, or any other trends and movement within the industry.

When you're starting out in this industry, pick head-hunters' brains for information about your region, but don't solely rely on them for placement. One serious benefit of getting hired without using a head-hunter is that you may be eligible to receive a signing bonus in lieu of your employer having to pay out a head-hunter. Instead of the company paying the head-hunter, they may offer the money to you as an incentive to start with them.

Key Strategies from This Chapter:

1. Your first objective when interviewing with people in the pharmaceutical sales industry should be to **secure a ride-along**.

2. **Head-hunters are great resources** for figuring out how competitive your salary is – think of them as "agents" for sales reps.

3. Before accepting a job offer from a head-hunter, **consider the hidden costs and risks** of the new position and ask yourself if you could secure the position without the head-hunter's help.

Chapter 7:
Salary and Other Considerations

What You'll Learn in This Chapter:

1. How not to blow your salary negotiation in an interview.

2. Topics and points to focus on in your interview.

3. The key mistake most people make when negotiating salary.

4. The often-overlooked pay elements that can add thousands of dollars to your salary.

The pharmaceutical industry is known for paying a very good salary, which is one of the main reasons people wish to enter it. There is such potential here that it's easy to get excited about getting your job and starting a career, then forget why you want to do all of this.

One thing I love about this industry is the people I meet. Every day I get to discuss problems and issues with everyone from neurosurgeons to pathologists to general practitioners. But at the end of the day, my job is a great way to give my wife and children a nice home, a warm bed, and plenty of good food - not to mention the odd trip to exotic places. If you want to do this, it is extremely important that you negotiate the best possible salary for yourself. This is not only important for your financial wellbeing, but also for creating a positive image and reputation that will add to your future career.

Nailing an Interview and Negotiating Starting Salary

Here is a personal story that illustrates the importance of developing your skills before you try to negotiate a salary for yourself.

When I landed an interview for a job as a high-level specialist for a large region, I could not have been more excited - or more prepared. When I walked into the hotel where my interview was to take place, I knew the background of every interviewer in the room. I was especially aware of the sales manager's strong drive to hire talented salespeople. He did not want a scientist; he was looking for a good salesperson.

Because of this, the interview went perfectly and he was very impressed. At one point he challenged me to sell one of the drugs I would be selling if I got the job. I did this without any prior knowledge of the drug itself, simply by asking him questions and keeping *efficacy, safety,* and *cost* in mind.

It was the end of the interview that really sealed the deal. I used the line that I introduced you to in Chapter 4: "After what we have discussed, do you believe that you are ready to offer me the job?"

The results of my using this line convinced me that I would never miss another opportunity to use it. The position was mine - I knew it and he knew it. On top of that, because of my strong selling approach I gained the respect from him that I would need later on when he was my superior and I was coming to him with issues and problems.

The funny part is that this is where the interview went south.

Without missing a beat, he asked me what salary I would need to come over to his division. For some reason, I responded by asking for $50,000, which really is an arbitrary number. Giving this number was the first and only mistake I made during the interview.

Of course, he immediately accepted. This is the kicker. Who knows how much he was willing to pay me? I did very well in the interview, so that reply could have cost me thousands of dollars every year. What if I had said $60K? Would he have said yes? I'll never know.

Rule to Remember:
The third rule of sales is "Whoever speaks first loses."

I spoke first and I lost. Over the years, that little mistake could have cost me thousands of dollars, not only in initial salary but in subsequent raises that are all based on a percentage. For example, with a $50,000 starting salary a 5% increase will take you to $52,500. But if you start at $60,000, a 5% increase will take you to $63,000. It makes a huge difference, as you can see, especially compounded over the years.

The Right Way to Negotiate Salary, Vacations, and Bonuses

In hindsight, what I should have done is ask my interviewer how much his specialist sales reps were making. This would have put the ball in his court and he would have spoken first. Though from what I know about him now he most likely would have turned the discussion to get me to give a number (he was a great mentor and salesman who taught me a lot of what I know). That is the fun of business negotiations.

Another thing you should not miss out on is negotiating for vacations. This is one area I would like to see increased. Personally, I would not hesitate to ask for four or five weeks of vacation.

When negotiating for your vacation time try to get a carry-over, which is a vacation that you are entitled to take any time after starting. When I started, I had to wait for an entire year before taking a vacation. It would have been nice to have three or four weeks to start with - and I am sure that all I had to do was ask.

Rule to Remember:
The first rule of sales is "Ask and you shall receive."

Another thing you should ask for is a signing bonus. These can be quite high - $10,000 would be fairly standard. This is especially true if you are not going through a head-hunter. Head-hunters are usually paid a percentage of your salary, which can mean tens of thousands of dollars of extra expenses for the company that is hiring you. If there is no head-hunter to collect on this, there may be an opportunity for you to keep some of this money for yourself. In the end, it all comes down to the first rule of sales: "Ask and you shall receive."

Key Strategies from This Chapter:

1. **Know what your employer is looking for** during an interview, and be sure to focus on that. In pharmaceutical sales, remember that *efficacy*, *safety*, and *cost* are three of the main factors in decision making.

2. Do everything you can to **avoid being the first one to name a price** when negotiating salary. Remember the third rule of sales: "Whoever speaks first loses." Instead, ask what specialist reps are earning at the company.

3. **Remember to consider bonuses and vacations** when negotiating salary. These benefits can really add up!

SECTION TWO:
OUT ON THE ROAD

Chapter 8:
Company Training

What You'll Learn in This Chapter:

1. What to expect when you begin training with your new company.

2. How efficacy, safety, and cost work together to help you develop your pitch.

3. Tips for submitting expenses.

4. Things to consider before using client management software.

Most likely the first thing to arrive when you are hired will be binders full of reading material. This may seem a little daunting at times, but do not worry. To be honest, few salespeople actually read and retain the bulk of this information. Real learning comes from being out on the road, and if your company training is good it also comes from the skilled people in your new head office.

I could go into how to dissect these papers and discuss different types of trials, but for now you should concentrate on reading the title and conclusion of each piece. I am not saying that these papers are not useful, but if these materials were all there is to selling pharmaceuticals, what purpose would sales reps serve? Companies could simply mail the papers to physicians to read - it sure would save them a lot of time.

Product Knowledge and Sales Training

After a couple of weeks of home study you will be off to your head office. In Canada most are located in Montreal, Pointe Claire, and Toronto. The US has a much larger population density so your training will be in a major city. There will be an intense two weeks of training sessions to teach you the ins and outs of selling pharmaceuticals or medical devices.

For the two weeks you will learn company policy regarding computers, cars, cell phones, voice mail, chain of command, medical affairs, and even how to expense your lunches. The meetings will briefly touch on everything that you will do on a day-to-day basis. The vast majority of your time will be spent dealing with product knowledge and sales training.

Developing Your Sales Pitch: Focus on Efficacy

People buy drugs for three main reasons. These reasons are efficacy, safety, and cost. The number one reason without a doubt is *efficacy*. Always make sure you focus on this before you even think of moving on to something else.

How well does your drug work? Has it been compared to another tried-and-true drug in a clinical trial or observation? What evidence do you have that your drug works?

Efficacy will almost certainly be the main focus of your sales pitch. Perhaps you will achieve this by sharing the results of a head-to-head trial between your product and a competing one. Perhaps you will do it by describing a "single-arm" study versus a placebo (such as a sugar pill) which shows some sort of advantage. What is the advantage of using your product instead of another?

Only if you have a situation where there is similar efficacy do you go to the next two reasons, which are *safety* and *cost*. These are important, but they are minor considerations in comparison to efficacy. For example, if your child had cancer and there was a magic pill that you knew would cure it, would you even consider *not* purchasing this product to cure your child? Efficacy is everything when it comes to purchasing products.

The last example is, of course, extreme. There is no magic pill. Talented salespeople shine at filling in all the grey areas between the black and white; we have to look at what evidence we have to help us make the best decision.

Safety: The Next Consideration in Developing Your Pitch

The second consideration in developing your pitch is *safety*.

How safe does a drug have to be in order for a doctor to use it? This is a huge issue in the selling and prescribing of pharmaceuticals and gets a lot of press, but of course the issue of drug safety has been around since physicians began using drugs to treat patients. To understand what a doctor is thinking when they prescribe a medication to a patient, one has only to remember some of the tragic examples in the past where people have been harmed and killed by pharmaceuticals. Thalidomide and the tragedy that occurred to pregnant women who used this drug is just one example in our history.

The physician's motto is "Do no harm." Drug safety is a life-and-death issue, and everyone involved in decisions about drug treatments must weigh the potential benefits of a pharmaceutical against its potential risks.

In some studies, patients are polled regarding the potential risk they would be willing to put up with for a particular benefit. For example, say you have cancer and there is a 100% chance that you will die of your disease. There is a drug you could take that will cure 99% of the people who take it. The catch is that 1% of people taking this drug die an instantaneous, painless death. Would you take it?

Most people would say yes to the above question. But the question is, where is your grey zone? Say there were a 90% chance of death from the disease, and the drug had a 90% cure rate but a 10% chance of instantaneous death. Most likely, you would still choose to use the drug in question.

Before your company training, it is a good idea to get to know some of your new colleagues and get an idea of what strategies, angles, and marketing materials they are currently using in their territories. These people are the ones who took you out on ride-alongs in the past, so you may have seen them use some of the marketing material. They will be able to give you a good idea what clinical studies you should be using to prove efficacy, safety, and cost.

Tracking Your Expenses

Computers are an integral part of all pharmaceutical selling situations these days. Most companies will expect you to come with a solid idea of what computers can do, so you should have general skills with e-mail, Word, Excel, and Outlook.

The computer training you receive from the head office will revolve more around your expense reporting system and client relation management systems. The expense reporter is a tool that helps you track all your expenses and send them into a main database for the master bill. It will usually give you a way to get a cheque cut from the main head office, automatically reimbursing you for your expenses.

The main software that is used these days is SAP (Systems Application and Products). It can handle everything from your expense reporting systems to getting cheques cut from the company to pay vendors you have hired.

Every two weeks, you will most likely have to spend an hour or two filling in every expense you have incurred during the last two weeks. Everything from your parking fees to hotel bills will get recorded and added up. After this you will submit your expenses by e-mail and within a few days, sometimes a week, the money will be deposited in your bank account.

Every company has different requirements for how you can submit expenses. In the last few years, this has become a very complex situation. More and more scrutiny has come to the corporate world - and with that scrutiny, the amount of paperwork has increased.

As a side note, if you can use a credit card to help you get points I would recommend this. It is a real perk from doing business.

Managing Clients and Using Contact Management Software

There has been an explosion in the development of CRM (Client Relationship Management) software in the past ten years. Companies usually have their own names for this software, but all the systems out there are fairly similar. They record the client's name, address, and all sorts of other information about them, with the intended purpose of helping you develop your interpersonal relations with your clients.

The main system that has been adopted by most outside sales force companies is called Salesforce (www.salesforce.com), which is web-based, all-encompassing software that will take you no time at all to figure out. It is an excellent way to keep clients' names, phone numbers, and addresses, though after selling for a year you will know who your main people are. You will not need a computer with a list, recording call times and notes. These programs are a client list, a "black book" if you will.

I have included the link to the website for Salesforce. Go have a look at the demo video it will give you a good idea of what this software can do.

These programs have to be used with intelligence, or they can make your interaction feel impersonal and fake. With my best clients I don't need to write points down because I remember what they tell me as I would remember it from a friend.

Use these tools as an aid to the business. Over the years I have seen a battle between management and sales representatives over the use of these programs. Some of them today can actually be linked up with GPS (Global Positioning Satellites) so that they can track the movements of the outside sales rep. The decision to invest heavily in these programs comes from way up in the chain of command, and many people have put much time and effort into them. Some people are very passionate about them. My feeling is that sitting in front of my client is what creates the relationship and makes the sale. Ultimately, this software is merely a tool helping you get to the core of the business.

Key Strategies from This Chapter:

1. **Avoid relying on sales literature**, and remember that you have been hired to use your selling skills. No matter how attractive the sales literature for a company's products may be, they have hired you because they need a person to sell those products face-to-face to other people.

2. **Efficacy, efficacy, efficacy!** Efficacy is everything in your pharmaceutical sales pitch. Safety and cost are important considerations, but they are only primary considerations in situations where a competing product has similar efficacy to yours.

3. Computers can be an indispensable tool for managing your expenses and client lists, but remember that they can only store and process information. It's up to you to develop real relationships with the people you work with.

Chapter 9:
Finding the Core of Your Business

What You'll Learn in This Chapter:

1. How to find the small group of customers who are responsible for 80% of your business.

2. The information source that lets you zero in on your best customers and identify ones that aren't being honest with you.

3. Three rules that help you generate maximum exposure for your product and maximize your sales.

4. The most powerful technique for winning new clients before you even speak with them.

Know Your Customers: The 80/20 Rule

To find real success in this industry you will need to be able to find out which clients are your busiest and highest-prescribing ones.

Rule to Remember:
***The fourth rule of sales states that "80% of your business will come
from 20% of your customers."***

The 80/20 rule applies not only to the pharmaceutical industry, but to every business out there. It is truly an integral part of success in any selling job, and more importantly it will help you focus your precious time on the people who are worth focusing on.

In Chapter One I discussed the importance of finding the decision makers within any company. These are the people whose opinions are most respected. If they want something done, it is usually done. And just as there are decision makers in every pharmaceutical company, there are key decision makers throughout the medical profession.

In this chapter you will get a few tricks to help you discover who these people are. It is time to get out the sleuthing hat, because it is amazing where they hide. I have watched groups operate where the CEO or the Chair of the meeting really doesn't use their power and all of the decision-making is left up to people who report into them. This is actually a powerful business strategy and shows that the leaders have a lot of faith in their people.

Using Prescription or "Doctor-Level" Data

More and more companies these days are finding that using information about prescription methods is a quick and easy method for finding decision makers within the medical community. There are quite a few sources that sell what is called "doctor-level data," or prescription data.

This information comes from pharmacies, or businesses that purchase the data from pharmacies, which track every prescription a doctor writes. You will get a monthly or quarterly readout or database telling you how many times Dr. Jones used your product, or your competitor's product.

This is important information, as it can quickly and accurately give you up-to-date data on some very important clients. A good salesperson is always looking to get more information about clients and the business, though often when they first read it they will already know much of the information.

You should be aware that some companies do not bother collecting or disclosing this information and it is even unavailable in certain areas and from certain companies. For example, Wal-Mart does not disclose any prescription data in Canada (I am not sure if they do in the USA).

This data is also very expensive, so some companies do not wish to pay for it. This decision may well be a good one - good salespeople know the business and the pharmacies, and in that case may not need such data. Ultimately it will depend on the amount of revenue that the brand you are selling is bringing in. If the investment is worth it, then the information may be available.

In some territories, physicians have got together to ensure that companies cannot purchase this information. This can create issues between clients and salespeople, as you don't ever want to be confrontational with clients. Sometimes you may be told by a client that they are using your product when you know from your doctor-level data that this is not the case. When this happens, make sure that you always keep a professional attitude - tact and persuasion are always the best methods to use.

Regardless, you cannot rely only on this data. In some situations, this information is not going to help you make a sale. When pharmaceutical decisions are made on a hospital Pharmacy and Therapeutics Committee, for example, the people on this committee are not necessarily the ones who will actually write the prescriptions, though they can, through their influence, make decisions which will allow for many others to use pharmaceutical products.

There are really two types of core doctors: "prescribers" and "influencers." You will see this distinction all the time when you are working in the industry. I have sat in many a grand round or regular round and seen a surgeon, a pharmacist, or even a nurse dictate which drugs will be used and which will not be used. These people are influencers.

A "Grand Rounds" is typically a large meeting with in the hospital with a key speaker or group of speakers. This meeting is attended by a large audience that can include all types of HCP (Health Care Practitioner's). For example the audience may range from General Surgeons, to Family Medicine specialists to nurses, pharmacists and pathologists. A regular rounds would be smaller in scale and targeted to a more specific group. For example general surgery might have a set a rounds and only this group. In attendance other than general surgeons for these might be nurses and pharmacists that assist the general surgeons in their day to day operations.

The general rule is that a specialist physician will dictate or suggest what general practitioners should do or prescribe. This is not always the case; very experienced GPs are very influential. In other cases, nurses will tell physicians what to prescribe.

Through all of this, while you are learning about who is prescribing what and who the influencers are and who the prescribers are, talk to everyone, gather information, and ask questions. Through all of your meetings and information gathering, your product will naturally gain exposure.

Generating Product Exposure and Maximizing Your Sales

This highlights one more excellent rule.

Rule to Remember:
The fifth rule of sales is "The best way to sell is to have someone else do it for you."

When managing your core contacts, a key strategy is to create situations where one physician is selling to other physicians. This can be done in a dinner, lunch, or breakfast meeting.

As you are asking questions and gathering information, don't waste your time out there selling to people who are not going to (a) write prescriptions for your product or (b) have any influence over the care of the patient. In other words, don't bother trying to sell your drug to someone who can't use it. I found my typical target list for information sources to be nurses, pharmacists, doctors, specialists, other salespeople, and secretaries.

Rule to Remember:
The sixth rule of sales is "Don't preach in the desert."

Pharmacists are an excellent source of information about products, physicians, and physician's prescribing habits. These are, after all, the people who give your products to the patient, so pay some special attention to them.

Also, if a pharmacist is out of stock of one of your competitor's products and a prescription comes in for this product, they can make a phone call and ask the doctor to make a switch if they have your product in stock. This kind of opportunity comes up often, so be sure to take advantage of it whenever possible.

Of course, the same thing can also happen to you. It is up to you to make sure that your pharmacies are fully loaded with a lot of your product so this scenario will never happen to you. Remember that a fully stocked customer is a loyal customer.

Be sure to convince your pharmacists about the merits of your drug and get them believing in the efficacy of the product. If you are successful in convincing them, it only makes sense that they will then share the names and information of a number of core doctors in the region that they see a lot of scripts from.

Your Clients Sell Products For You

When you spend your time convincing a client to use your product, you are effectively recruiting them as part of your sales force. When they discover the benefits of your product, they may refer it to their colleagues, helping you make additional sales.

Rule to Remember:
The seventh rule of sales is "One sale gives you more sales."

Here is an example of this rule in action: the other day my wife was on the phone with a salesperson trying to sign us up for a long-distance plan. In the end, she agreed to switch long-distance providers because she liked the service and the flat rate they were offering for calls within North America. My wife liked the plan so much that she started phoning every single one of her friends and telling them about the plan.

At one point, I told her that she should go and get a job with the company because she was so passionate about their plan. She was even following up with her friends to make sure that they had switched over! In effect, by making a sale this company had gained a free salesperson.

Once someone is convinced of the value of a product, they want to tell the whole world about it. It's human nature; we want others to think like us.

The Power of Positive Referrals

So how does this story relate to pharmaceutical sales? Well, if one doctor is convinced of the value of your product they may give you more contacts to call on. The sweet part of this is that you then walk through the door of your potential new client with a referral from a respected colleague of theirs.

Nurses and office managers often play key roles in referring new contacts, and they can give you all sorts of information. These people are also aware of what specialists a physician will refer to in the area.

Once you gain a new referral to a physician, a helpful first step is to figure out the type of patient this particular physician sees. For example, the physician might have a large elderly population or a large female population in their practice. The female population would be prime candidates for birth control pills, or if you were selling incontinence drugs you would target the doctor with elderly patients.

Nurses are especially important in the hospital setting. They know a great deal about the inner workings of the hospital. If you are having a terrible time with one of your clients who is very hard to deal with, nine times out of ten the nurses will feel the same way. I would even suggest that the patients do as well.

One of my clients, a physician I was selling chemotherapy to, was very difficult to make appointments with. He would pass me by without a glance and hardly return my hello, let alone allow me to book an appointment with him. I went to speak with some of the nurses who I knew quite well and had a good relationship with, and they informed me that they had had the same experience and found him to be a rude man with terrible interpersonal skills. The worst part was that the patients thought this as well. The nurses had a hard time watching how the patients reacted, having to deal with this type of physician.

One of my clients teaches doctors, and he once told me that can always tell which ones are going to be great doctors: the ones with the lowest academic marks. The doctors who are easy to talk to and have great bedside manners, who can get the patient to open up and share all of their problems - these are usually the ones who did not hit the books as much, because they enjoy human interaction versus academia.

Of course, this is just a general rule and hardly applies to all cases. Still, if you are having an easy conversation with a physician, you can bet everyone does too, from the nurse to the patient. Personable, sociable clients are influential because of their people skills. That being said, I have also seen the opposite hold true, where a nasty person holds incredible power.

It is difficult for me to overemphasize the importance of influencers when you are trying to make a sale. One of my colleagues used to work as an encyclopaedia salesman, and a favorite strategy of his was to go to a small town and immediately visit the town pastor or priest and leave him an encyclopedia to review for the evening. The next day, he would say, "I can leave you with this book; would you agree that the children of your town would benefit from it?" Of course the answer was yes every time, and from then on my friend would have a very influential figure in the community endorsing his product.

There is nothing more satisfying than walking into a physician's office with a recommendation from their colleague down the hall or even across town. In Chapter 14 you will learn more about how you can set up situations where one doctor will sell to a number of other doctors. This is a very powerful way to influence the medical community, and it works on the same principle that has my wife phoning all our friends about the telephone plan.

Key Strategies from This Chapter:

1. It's a rule: **80% of your business comes from 20% of your customers.** Learn who these customers are and focus your efforts on them.

2. Prescription or "doctor-level" data can be a great tool for learning who is using your products, but use this data with discretion if it is available to you.

3. **Know the difference between "prescribers" and "influencers,"** and be sure to approach both groups.

4. Remember the seventh rule of sales: **"One sale gives you three others."** A satisfied customer will sell your products for you by giving enthusiastic recommendations to their friends and colleagues. Never underestimate the power of positive referrals!

Chapter 10:
Access to Your Clients

What You'll Learn in This Chapter:

1. How to approach doctors.

2. The three main types of interaction you'll have with doctors, and how to make the most of each.

Access to your clients is key to your success, and it is a part of selling that many salespeople agonize over. Failure to gain access not only makes for a tough day, but will also limit the number of prescriptions that you can generate.

Initial Considerations when Setting Up Doctor Meetings

If a doctor is very easy to see, you can be sure that they are also receiving visits from every other salesperson in the area, so the benefits of your visit are likely to be tempered. When you are starting out selling to GPs or family doctors, make note of the hard-to access doctors and be persistent in visiting them, but take them in small doses. This job will eat you alive if you spend your days trying to see people who do not like you or want to meet with you. I once read a really interesting article about one of the last door-to-door Fuller Brush salesmen. His strategy was to go and see a number of his loyal customers (people that gave him a real sense of happiness to be around) throughout the day. He would also fit in a couple of difficult or harder to access people each day. This way the majority of his experiences were positive but he still got a couple of challenges in as well.

Another benefit of seeing the easier to reach people is that you will be able to perfect your sales presentation and learn how to sell pharmaceuticals more effectively. Practice makes perfect. This way when you get in to see the harder to reach people your sales pitch will be dynamite!

That said, hard-to-see physicians can really make a difference because if you are having trouble meeting with them, you can bet that many other people are as well. This can make for less competition. One effective way to access these people is through their peers. As I mentioned before, a great opening line can be: "Dr. Jones, I am glad to see you. Dr. Davey down the hall told me how important it is that I speak with you."

Generally, there are three types of interactions you will be trying to achieve:

1. The sit-down call.
2. The hallway chat or "sample-cupboard detail."
3. The breakfast/lunch/dinner meeting.

Interaction #1: Sit-Down Call

The sit-down call is by far the most effective method for meeting with doctors. When I am doing the hallway chat or sample-cupboard detail (which I will describe in a minute), I always try to get a sit-down. For example I will ask, "Would you be able to sit for a few minutes and discuss some details about the treatment of hypertension? If you are busy, perhaps I could set up an appointment with you at a later date with your secretary."

I always work toward booking a sit-down call, because in order to get a doctor discussing patient management a call should last from 30 minutes to an hour. This may sound like a lot of time, but you will know what I am talking about the moment a doctor gets out a patient's chart to discuss the possibility of using your drug to treat one of his or her patients.

Of course this will not happen with every doctor on every call, but it is a good goal and the most effective way to sell pharmaceuticals. Good patient management discussions are the key to learning where your drug or product fits within a doctor's practice.

This may not happen to you so much selling to GPs, but it will happen more as you move into specialist sales and get better at bringing GPs out of their shells. This type of meeting leaves you with a good feeling, and confirms to you that you can help your clients.

Interaction #2: Hallway Chat/Sample-Cupboard Detail

Any time you meet with a client briefly in a hallway, at a sample cupboard, or even in an elevator, you can mention something about your product. This brief conversation is a "hallway chat." It often happens at the sample cupboard (for example, if you are dropping off some samples of a drug and the doctor is grabbing some aspirin for a patient) so it is sometimes referred to as the "sample-cupboard detail."

This type of interaction is useful, but in the end its purpose is simply to reinforce a point. We discussed earlier how many times you would have to tell a physician a dosage before feeling comfortable that they would remember it. Five times is the minimum, but the more the better.

Time and time again, I have had physicians tell me that the only reason they were not using my product was that they had forgotten. When this is the case, the hallway chat then becomes more of a habit-breaking exercise.

An excellent strategy for breaking these habits is to come up with a quick one-liner describing the recommended dosage for a product you are selling. If physicians should be prescribing 100 milligrams of Drug X for 100 days, work the phrase "a hundred for a hundred" into your sample-cupboard detail. This example would be especially effective if your product comes in packages of 100 capsules. Repetition, repetition, repetition is the key to selling your products.

For example, can you recite the seven rules of sales from memory yet? I bet you need to look them up. Here they are again:

- **Rule #1: Ask and you shall receive.**

- **Rule #2: Two ears, one mouth.**

- **Rule #3: Whoever speaks first loses.**

- **Rule #4: The 80/20 rule.**

- **Rule #5: The best way to sell is having someone sell for you.**

- **Rule #6: Do not preach in the desert.**

- **Rule #7: One sale gives you three others.**

Rules number five and seven go hand in hand. One buyer, once fully convinced, will tell all their friends about their great buy, and will try to convince those friends to seek out the same bargain they found.

I will say it again: repetition is an effective way to get your product into the mind of a physician. Hallway chats are ideal opportunities to repeat your message, but also keep in mind that your goal is to sit for 45 minutes or so to discuss treatment details with a physician.

Interaction #3: Breakfast/Lunch/Dinner Meeting

The last type of client access meeting is the breakfast, lunch, or dinner meeting. These are as good as a sit-down meeting, as you will have at least an hour to discuss business. Over the years, I have found that these meetings are an excellent way to sell pharmaceuticals. Food has a calming effect on people, and they tend to become disarmed.

As long as this strategy is not abused it can be very effective, but if you begin to feel more like a caterer than a salesperson it is probably time to cut down on the number of meals you are giving away. I often see situations where a doctor is using a salesperson to feed his staff as a staff perk, and only giving the salesperson a quick two minutes to talk about the product.

Be honest enough to admit to yourself, "I don't believe that this meeting is bringing us closer to the goal of discussing disease management and figuring out where a product might help a patient."

Doctors are quite interesting in many different areas, and I have found them to be fantastic conversationalists. The number of meal meetings you schedule will depend on how much time you are willing to spend doing this. Remember the potential work hours of this job.

Dinner meetings are usually more social in nature. These are not to be confused with Continuing Medical Education (CME) programs. A CME program is an event with a respected keynote speaker giving a brief (usually one-hour) education session, and usually involves a specialist delivering a presentation to a number of other physicians.

Key Strategy:
An evening presentation by a keynote speaker with a favorable
impression of your product is an excellent way to promote a pharmaceutical.

I often laugh because the industry gets such scrutiny over meals. You would think that the only way disease management discussion should happen would be in a white room with no windows. It is really hard to convince people to leave their families and friends for an evening to discuss patient management on their own time, and putting people in a white room with no windows isn't going to help.

Key Strategies from This Chapter:

1. **Make note of hard-to-access doctors**. If you're having trouble with them, chances are that other sales reps are striking out with them too! Practice your pitch on easier prospects, then move in to crack these tough nuts.

2. **A sit-down meeting should be your goal** for every doctor interaction, but in reality you'll be having lots of hallway chats too. Remember that the average person needs to hear the name of a product five times to remember it. Keep plugging away and get that sit-down meeting.

3. Meals can be a great way to get one-on-one time with a doctor, but **set boundaries on your time** and the number of meal meetings you schedule. Don't let doctors come to think of you as a caterer – keep your meetings focused on business.

Chapter 11:
Gathering Information within Your Territory

What You'll Learn in This Chapter:

1. Tips for gathering prescription data about your product and competing products.

2. How competitive Continuing Medical Education (CME) data can give you ideas to use within your territory.

3. The benefits of collecting competitive sales and marketing pieces, and where to find them.

4. How to gain new clients and keep on top of current ones.

Knowledge is power! The more information that you have about your territory, the more power you will have to change things within it.

In Chapter 9 I discussed "doctor-level" prescription data. This is a very important type of information that can guide you in your day-to-day activities as a sales rep, but there are many other types of information that can help you as well.

Monitoring the Competition through Sales and Marketing Pieces

You can learn a lot about your territory by monitoring the activity of your competitors. Other companies' competitive practices can give you a range of information about new and innovative strategies you could be using. Access to their client lists can come in handy as well, as you may also be able to sell your product to their clients.

During your travels and while visiting clinics and hospitals, get your hands on all the marketing tools you can find. The industry invests many millions of dollars into producing these pieces. Gather them up, as they can give you some fantastic insights into what strategies other companies are using to lure doctors into prescribing their products.

These pieces can also give your marketing team new ideas, and let them know what the competition is doing so as to produce a competitive answer to the strategy.

Gathering Information from CME Data, Nurses, and Pharmacists

Continuing Medical Education (CME) data can also be a great source of new ideas for you. For example, you can use it to gain information about specialists that other companies might be bringing in as key speakers, or about key supporters of these companies.

In the end, the key to gaining knowledge about your territory is to always be listening to your clients and the people that they deal with closely. One of my favourite strategies for finding a doctor's prescription habits is simply to talk with his or her receptionist. Quite often, these people transcribe the notes and charts of the patients from a doctor's dictation.

When speaking with a receptionist do not ask about the particulars of any patient's information, of course, as this would be a breach of confidence. However, asking a quick question like, "So, do you ever have to dictate the word [Drug XYZ]?" might give you just enough information to know if you are successful or not.

Nurses are another great source of information, as they are always spending time with physicians and their patients. They can often have an impact on drug prescriptions, either through writing simple prescriptions themselves or through influence they may have with the doctor.

Pharmacists can give you just as much information as the nurses, as they are the people that are dispensing the drugs. They may know the prescribing habits of any doctor out there, as long as it is within their interest to find and remember this information.

If you ever find yourself wondering how to approach these people for this information, simply remind yourself of the first rule of sales.

Rule to Remember:
The first rule of sales is "Ask and you shall receive."

Key Strategies from This Chapter:

1. **Monitor the activity of competing companies.** A great way to do this is by collecting marketing materials they use. Companies put big money into these products, and they can yield great insights into possible strategies that you, or your company, could be using.

2. **Use CME data as an information source.** This data can teach you a lot about strategies and specialists that other companies are using.

3. Don't forget about nurses and pharmacists! Nurses often influence doctors' prescribing decisions, and sometimes write prescriptions themselves. And pharmacists will often know a surprising amount about the prescribing habits of doctors in your territory.

SECTION THREE:
SELLING SKILLS

Chapter 12:
Open with a Greeting

What You'll Learn in This Chapter:

1. The reason most people are uncomfortable meeting with sales reps.

2. The four-part acronym you can use to quickly and easily put any person at ease when meeting them.

The sales process begins when you greet your client. The most important thing at this point is to make your client feel at ease. People need to feel comfortable.

Shared History Helps You Open Conversations

Opening new conversations gets easier as you progress in your profession. Over time you will gather more stories to tell, and will begin to build a rapport with your current client base.

History is a very important aspect of any relationship. Think of your best friends and what makes the conversation flow so well with these people - shared history.

About three months ago, I went back to my hometown for a visit. I had not been for quite some time, and I soon met up with a friend from high school who I had not seen in years. Within minutes we were catching up and it was like no time had passed. History plays a large part in relationships such as this one. If ever there was a break in conversation (as there is in any conversation) we always had the opportunity to talk about experiences we had shared in the past.

People Are Uncomfortable with Strangers

When you first start dealing with your clients you are not going to have any shared history, so it will be more difficult for you to have an easy conversation. At this stage you will likely find it helpful to rely upon some of the tricks I will reveal in this chapter.

The purpose of a greeting is really to disarm your client a little bit. When a stranger approaches, most people are immediately on guard. Think of how you feel when a street person walks up to you and asks you for money. This is not a flattering comparison, but it reveals something about how new clients are likely to feel when you approach them.

For another example, think of walking into an electronics dealership. A salesperson will approach and ask, "Is there anything that I can help you with?" This will immediately put you on guard, unless you really do need some questions answered.

In the same way, your clients know that you are in their office for a reason. For you to achieve any success in selling it is essential that you help your clients get past this initial uncomfortable feeling.

Of course, the same applies with regard to your enjoyment of your career. Imagine feeling uncomfortable for days and months as you meet all these new clients! A comfortable greeting will put both you and your clients at ease.

Use FORE to Build Rapport

Here is a trick I use to get past any uncomfortable moments when greeting a new client. It's a word used by golfers all the time: "FORE!"

I use the word "FORE" as an acronym to remember the four main passions in people's lives:

- Family
- Occupation
- Recreation/Charity
- Entertainment

When I first walk into a doctor's office, I immediately begin looking at what they have displayed on their walls. This is a good exercise to practice when you walk into anyone's home or office. What do they have on display? Pictures of their family? A mountain range? Sailing? Golf?

You can learn an amazing amount about a person by inspecting the pictures and other items on display in their home or office. If they are going to put it up on their wall to look at every day, you can imagine how special a picture is to them.

When I see something that catches my interest, I will open the conversation with a question or comment about it. I love people and feel that they all have something to teach me. I take a genuine interest in their lives; this shows through and is a great way to break the ice. I also find that the books on their shelves can also tell you a lot about a person, like what they are interested in and spend a lot of time looking at.

A word of warning, though: if you don't have a genuine interest that's fine, but don't try to fake it as it really can backfire on you. Find something that really does interest you, then use that as a starting point for your conversation.

One of my life's passions is my **family**. When I walk into a client's office and see a picture of the client with their kids and spouse smiling under the Eiffel Tower in Paris, conversation naturally flows around this. I have been to Paris, so my client and I can compare notes, and I can tell my client that I would love to go back and see Paris again with my family.

Talk with your client for half an hour about their family and their adventures though life, and you will gain not only a new client, but a new friend.

Occupation is another main passion for many people, as we spend so much of our day doing it. How is your client's business going on a general level? Do they have any new partners? Are they involved in any professional development courses?

The same goes for **recreation** and **entertainment**. You could spend hours in conversation about these topics, as pretty much everyone likes to talk about what they do for fun.

If a client really doesn't want to chat about these topics, don't be alarmed. Some people are just very businesslike. They are thinking, "I don't like all this mushy nonsense. Why are you here? Show me what you have to show me and let me get back to what I do best, which is seeing patients and fixing their problems."

Fair enough. If you have one of these clients, don't push it; get down to business.

In general, though, from the beginning of your conversation with a client, don't rush it. If there is a small gap in the conversation, think: "Family, Occupation, Recreation, Entertainment." Don't worry about getting to business too quickly; it always comes up.

Key Strategies from This Chapter:

1. **Most people are uncomfortable when meeting strangers**, especially if those strangers are salespeople. It's up to you to start each meeting with a greeting that puts the other person at ease... your job depends on it!

2. **Use FORE (Family, Occupation, Recreation/Charity, Entertainment)** to open a conversation about something that the other person is interested in.

3. Don't just use formulas or prefab speeches to open a conversation. **Treat each contact like a person** and inquire about things that are important to them. That way, you'll be sure to build lasting relationships.

Chapter 13:
Probing through a Patient Profile

What You'll Learn in This Chapter:

1. The most effective way to move from opening the conversation to talking about products.

2. The key question you need to ask before you can start describing your solution.

After you open a conversation with a client, there will usually be a bridge in the conversation where you move from the greeting to talking about business. The key is to have this transition occur naturally. For the most part it generally happens naturally when your physician asks, "What brings you in today?"

Using Questions to Find the Treatment Algorithm

At this point in the conversation, I start asking questions and listening to the answers. If you remember the seven rules of sales, this is where Rule Number Two comes in: two ears, one mouth. Listen, listen, listen!

The questions I ask are always in line with disease management. This means that I am *not* going to spend my time discussing my product, but discussing the disease or problem that my product will fix, cure, or have an indication for.

If I am selling a drug for the treatment of acute sinusitis, I will ask questions about the number of patients the doctor sees with this problem. What is his preferred treatment algorithm for these patients? How does the client determine that a patient does indeed have a particular illness? Your clients can - and probably will - talk for hours about these topics.

Industry Tip:
A "treatment algorithm" is the typical course of treatment
a doctor follows when a patient comes in with a particular problem.

If a client ever asks why I am asking these questions, I usually answer that it is for our market research, so as to better understand our marketplace. Inquiring about the treatment algorithm is an absolutely fantastic open-ended question which reveals many aspects of a doctor's practice.

For example, a typical treatment algorithm for breast cancer would begin with the patient receiving a mammogram, learning that she has a tumour, and then going through surgery to have it removed. The surgeon then removes a certain margin around the tumour to eliminate the possibility of residual disease. Once the patient is disease-free, what type of adjuvant therapy will the doctor use? CEF (Cyclophosphamide, Epirubicin, 5Flourouricil)? AC (Adrimycin, Cyclophosphamide)? TAC (Taxane, Adriamycin, Cyclophosphamide)? What is the doctor's first choice of product? How would they improve on the product? What do they like about the product?

As you gain experience, you will begin thinking of these questions before visits with a particular doctor. They will be aimed at finding out the treatment pattern your doctor follows and, more importantly, *why* they choose to use these treatments.

Probing to Learn More about the Treatment Algorithm

Once you have gained this information about a doctor's treatment algorithm, you have hopefully brought the conversation around to the topic of an area in which your drug may work.

If you have not done so, re-evaluate the type of questions you are asking. Here are a few you might use:

- Has the client used or prescribed the drug before?
- Why did they choose it?
- What is the best way to describe the patients that your client is treating with this drug?
- What symptoms did the patients present that made the client choose this drug?
- Would they consider using this drug again if a similar patient walked in?
- Do they have patients on this drug because it was recommended by a specialist they trust?

There are a large number of questions that you could ask your client. Feel free to think up some more.

The title of this chapter is "Probing," which is what we are doing, but remember that the best way to do this is to listen to your client's answers to your questions - really listen and don't assume.

Listening carefully can be the hardest part of your client interaction. I find this especially so when I have been selling for a long time to a number of clients. It is always interesting for me to work with a colleague, accompanying them into a call with a client I have already called on thirty times. I may think that I know exactly what the client is going to say, but sure enough my colleague will start to ask some great new questions and all of this new information comes out.

When I would go on field visits with sales reps that reported to me, one of the most common things they would do is assume they knew the answers to questions. This can cause problems because as soon as you think you already know the answer, you could stop listening to what a client is really saying. Fight against this. It is especially true of people that have been selling for a while because they feel that they have heard it all before.

Over time you will learn more about the disease site that your drug works in by probing in this way. You have a lot to learn from your clients; it is important to remember that they are extremely intelligent and highly educated people. For the most part, they also like to teach and explain. When someone goes to school for as long as they have, they become proud of their knowledge and want to show it off. They are also interested in learning more.

The sharing of knowledge is the bridge to the next step of the sales call, which is the presentation. From all of this probing, you have learned what treatment algorithm your client is using and what problems they may be experiencing. You also have a good idea of the factors that might make the doctor purchase a product: efficacy, limited side effects, symptom control, or many other key factors. Next, it's time to put what you've learned together into an effective guided presentation.

Key Strategies from This Chapter:

1. After you have opened the conversation with a greeting, **don't jump right into talking about your products.** Instead use questions to encourage doctors to describe treatments they are using and prescribing.

2. When you have begun to identify the treatment algorithm a doctor is using, **continue using questions to probe about efficacy.** If there is a need for your product, this will uncover it, and your job of selling the product will be much easier.

Chapter 14:
Guided Presentations

What You'll Learn in This Chapter:

1. The difference between point-of-sale and long-term sales, and why it matters in pharmaceutical sales.

2. The key tactic for winning long-term formulary sales.

3. Tips and techniques for coping with the ups and downs of long-term selling.

4. How to prepare and deliver an effective guided presentation.

At this point in your sales call you have had a great opening and the discussion has moved on to your physician's pattern of practice. You have discussed disease types along with current treatment algorithms and options that are available.

Through a guided presentation you can demonstrate areas where your drug might help the physician. For example, if they have used it in the past but seen side effects, this is an objection that you can manage through a guided presentation.

The key to an effective sales presentation is to have a calm, step-by-step approach. Rome was not built in a day.

Point-Of-Sale Versus Long-Term Sales

Pharmaceutical selling is an interesting type of sales because it is both a point-of-sale interaction and a long-term sales process.

An example of a point-of-sale interaction might be buying a stereo. There is some discussion with a salesperson involved, and maybe you do a little research about what model you would like, but ultimately the discussion to buy is made on the spot. You pay for your new stereo, the salesperson upsells you on the speaker wires, and you take it home. Sure, you may read a couple of brochures, but when it comes down to it you are going to walk into a store and walk out with a product - or not.

Long-term selling is different in that the buying decision is usually not in the hands of only one individual. It takes longer to convince all the players, and the amount of money involved is considerably greater. With this type of selling it is important to have all the key players at the table supporting your product so that in the end there are no objections from any of the main people involved in the decision-making process.

Winning the Formulary Sale

This type of long-term sale is best described as a "formulary" decision. Pharmaceuticals are used extensively in hospitals, and having your drug on the formulary can result in a huge number of sales. This happens not just from the sale of the drug to the hospital itself, but also to patients over the long term. If a patient leaves the hospital but remains on your product the sales are likely to continue, as patients are rarely switched off to another product after leaving the hospital.

I had one account take two years before they finally made the move to switch the formulary and give me the sale. When I first approached the group with the idea to move the product up the treatment algorithm to the first line, there was strong resistance. The objections included everything from efficacy (they did not believe that it was a better product) to cost (they felt it was not worth the extra expense even if there was a small benefit). These reasons and many others were expressed as explanations of why they would not bring the drug onto the formulary.

It was a slow and steady battle trying to convince all the key people that the drug was worth the expense and did help the patients. When they were all sitting around the table, I didn't want any of them to raise objections. If someone did, I wanted four others to explain why the objection was wrong.

Rule to Remember:
*The fifth rule of sales is "The best way to sell is to
have someone else do it for you."*

In the end my persistence resulted in a visit to one of my key players and I was informed that they had decided that "the data" supported using my product as the first-line treatment. Sales went up by $1.5 million dollars overnight.

Preparing for the Ups and Downs of Long-Term Selling

When you sell pharmaceuticals, there is almost no recognition of the work you do by your clients. The reason for this is simple. They are the ones in the end that decide to put the patient on the drug. You facilitate this but the reality is that they make the ultimate decision.

When you are selling to GPs or Family Medicine, you might visit five clients on a good day. Some days you might have only one or two successes with your clients during the day. Those two successes will build over time, day after day, and as a result two things will happen.

First, your sales will go up in a steady increase day after day. When I started selling in this industry, I was very keen and worked like crazy. This is the approach I would recommend when you are starting out. It will teach you the business quickly. I started out putting in 12-hour days and seeing as many clients as I could. Many days, I would see 20 doctors in one day. After a few months my sales started to come in, and to my horror they were flat. There was a little growth, but not much.

How could all of this work not result in an increase in my sales? Were my clients lying to me?

I asked my mentor, and he assured me that I was doing a fantastic job. He told me to give it some time before expecting anything great. Sure enough, a few months later there was a steady growth in the number of sales I was making.

The second and most important thing that will happen as your successes build is that these accomplishments will keep you going. On any day you might receive four rejections, but your one or two successes will keep you coming back. At the end of the day, you will sit back and think about that one great call you had right at the end of the day. This is what keeps your spirits up.

Long-term sales can take years, and the many setbacks you encounter can give your morale a beating, but at the end you are rewarded with one large sale which gives you a big boost in morale when the big deal finally closes. The hard part comes when you realize that this success is fairly short-lived and does not seem to reward you for very long.

A supportive boss is essential throughout this process, as they can really boost your morale and help you pace yourself for the long haul. They also can give you a number of new ideas when you think that you are drained and that there is nothing new that can be done.

Preparing the Perfect Guided Presentation

Both long-term sales and point-of-sale interactions involve a presentation of your products. These presentations are often described as "canned" or "scripted," but they simply cannot come off as such. The challenge will come when you have sold a particular client five times in the past and you feel that if you launch into your canned script one more time, he might throw you out of his office.

It is a good idea to have a "perfect" presentation down so that you can quote all the necessary figures from memory. Armed with this ideal sales call, use the knowledge you gained earlier in this section about sales management to see which part or parts will work best.

Discussion of disease management is the key to this type of selling. Don't rush into the presentation, as it usually comes up naturally at some point in the sales call. It has to, as your product will fit into that doctor's treatment of the disease.

Once the presentation is finished, the next step is to handle any objections that may arise. No "perfect" presentation is actually going to nail it every time - there have to be some objections in any successful sale.

Key Strategies from This Chapter:

1. Pharmaceutical sales combine elements of point-of-sale and long-term selling. Be prepared to put a lot of effort into winning the big victories.

2. The best way to win big-time formulary sales is to get as many of the stakeholders on your side as possible, then **let them do the selling for you.** This takes time and a lot of relationship building, but it's how the big players in the industry make the big sales.

3. **Celebrate each victory,** and don't let little objections and rejections get to you. You're in this for the long term, so keep the big picture in focus.

4. **Don't rush into your guided presentation,** but have it ready to bring out when your prospect is ready for it. Keep disease management as the focus of the interaction.

Chapter 15:
Handling Objections

What You'll Learn in This Chapter:

1. Why objections are a necessary part of every sale.

2. The best way to deal with "red herring" objections.

3. Two steps for eliminating objections one by one.

4. How to know when you're ready to ask for the commitment.

When it comes to objections, the first thing to get your head around is that you *do* want to hear them. An objection is a positive sign that your doctor is considering your drug, and is looking for answers to questions or concerns they may have.

Finding the True Objection

The very worst scenario is a client who tells you over and over again that they love the drug and use it all the time, when in reality you know that they never use it. It is easy to uncover a scenario like this, as you never see the doctor's prescriptions in your sales or prescription data.

I had one client who told me every time I saw him how much he loved my drug, that it was his drug of choice and he was using it for his patients. However, the sales we had from his hospital did not support this claim. There was some business coming from his hospital, but not nearly enough based on estimates of his patient load and demographics of the patient draw that this hospital should have had.

The interesting part is that this doctor was not being dishonest with me. Instead, his failure to prescribe my product was due to his idea of what patients the product should be used to treat. In his mind, he was giving me the business!

At that point I didn't know this, but what I did know was that I needed to find the *true objection*.

Getting Past "Red Herring" Objections

To find the true objection, I needed to ask open-ended questions and to get my client talking. A lot of initial objections are really "red herring" objections - that is, they are intended more to distract than to provide a legitimate reason why the client is not buying your product.

A red herring is basically a quick, simple, get-out-of-my-face kind of objection. These are often somewhat argumentative as well. One example of this would be "Marijuana should be legal because tobacco (which is just as unhealthy) is legal." An argument such as this does not address the moral and societal issue of legalizing a drug, but may serve as a distraction by bringing up the fact that *another* very harmful drug is legal.

Many red herring objections are simple and off the cuff. In pharmaceutical sales, the classic (and most frequent) red herring objection is "that is an expensive drug!" As you learned earlier in this book, the three main reasons that people purchase products - pharmaceuticals included - are efficacy, safety, and cost. Notice that cost is the last and the least important reason people purchase pharmaceuticals, yet you will hear it discussed first in many instances.

Using cost as an excuse not to buy is a red herring because if the physician really believed that the efficacy and safety were much better, they would believe that it was worth the money to their patients. You can be sure that a physician who brings up cost right away does not really believe in the efficacy or safety of your product.

Understanding and Overcoming Objections

So how can you work through red herrings and other objections to arrive at your client's true objection? I use the following two-step process:

Step 1: Ensure that you understand what the doctor is really saying.

When an objection comes, I have found the easiest way to deal with it is to begin by ensuring that you really understand what the doctor is saying.

Restate the objection. Ensure that you hear what they are saying, and not what you want them to be saying. There is a big difference, as I have learned. Not listening properly can lead to problems and wasted time.

Repeat the objection as clearly as possible in your own words: "Doctor, if I understand correctly, you do not believe that the added efficacy is worth the money for the patient?"

Step 2: Explore the objection further with questions as to the nature of the objection.

Once I feel confident that I understand the objection, I use more questions to explore the nature of the objection. Where does it come from? Another patient? Another doctor? The competitor? This probing lets me find out how serious the objection really is.

Say that a doctor tells you your drug causes nausea and vomiting as side effects. The first thing that you might think is, "I know from my product monograph that this is very rare - maybe it isn't the drug at all." If you turn around and tell your client this, it is not going to make you any friends.

Think of the scenario that the doctor may have been in. He has just confidentially put a patient on your drug, and the next day a distraught patient returned and accused the doctor of trying to poison her because she vomited all night. If you tell your doctor, "My drug doesn't cause nausea or vomiting," then the doctor will think that you are lying - or at very least, that you are very cold and unsympathetic.

Instead use open-ended questions to learn more about what has happened to cause the doctor to raise this objection. How many times have they experienced this problem? Could anything else be causing the problem? Have you tried your product on other patients, and if so what was the experience of those patients?

With each open-ended question you ask, the client is going to reveal more about the true objection. I have seen this work many times; the discussion either brings out the real objection, or better yet leads the client to talk through the problem and discover the correct answer.

Rule to Remember:
The second rule of sales is
"Two ears, one mouth (listen, listen, listen!)"

Ask some questions and listen. "Do you have any patients with excellent health plans who would not worry about the cost of a prescription? Would you consider using this medication for these patients?"

That last sentence is actually a very good "closing" or "commitment" statement, and I have used it with success many times. You will learn more about closing in the next chapter, but these two aspects of a sales call (handling objections and closing) are very closely linked. Your answer to the objection can end with a close to ensure that you have answered the objection.

You can accomplish this by presenting a scenario to your client that brings the issue to the individual level. "Say, for example, I were to walk in as your patient. I work for a company with a very good health plan that would be able to fully reimburse this product. Would you prescribe the product if this were the case?"

This kind of scenario removes the objection as an issue, and also brings the discussion onto a real level about real patients that the doctor might have in his practice. Once the true objection is removed, you are free to move on and deal with any remaining objections that may come up. At this point, safety may come up; perhaps your client does not feel comfortable with the product's side effects because of something a competitor has told him in the past.

Throughout the process of handling these remaining objections continue to ask probing, open-ended questions. If your client were to describe a patient that would be suitable for your product, what would that patient look like? If they cannot describe any type of patient, why can't they? The clinical trials and papers that you use to detail and sell your product can help guide you in this type of discussion; be sure to read the criteria for entry into the study.

Remember that although pharmaceutical companies make billions of dollars selling pharmaceuticals to millions of people all over the world, your job is to relate a company's information to your doctor so that they understand when they should use your product. When a patient comes to your client pleading for help, you want your client to be able to offer your product to help the patient.

Turning Objections into New Questions

If you get stuck while handling an objection, here is a good strategy that works like a charm: turn it around!

Simply ask, "What do you think the answer to your problem could be?" This often gets a client talking, and better yet, thinking.

One benefit of selling pharmaceuticals is that your clientele are extremely smart. (For the most part, anyway - you will come across some clients who will make you wonder how they ever became doctors.) While they are thinking and talking, you get more time to gather information and think of new statements and angles where your product can fit into the disease group.

This is a huge benefit of having a doctor speak to you about their practice: you don't have to think as fast as you would during a silence!

Eliminate All Objections before Looking for the Commitment

One word of caution: you must eliminate all objections before you move to the next step, which is a commitment.

If you jump the gun, you can actually take a step backward and add more objections. Don't let your clients get the impression that you are trying to sell them a bill of goods without merit. Take the time to work through all the objections, *then* move on and ask for the commitment.

Key Strategies from This Chapter:

1. **Objections are a sign that a doctor is considering your solution,** and they are a necessary part of every sale. Take each objection seriously and learn how to deal with them confidently, one at a time.

2. When confronted with a "red herring" objection such as cost, **use questions to get at the true objection behind the red herring**, then resolve it.

3. **To deal with a legitimate objection, first restate it to make sure you understand it**, then ask questions about the nature of the objection. Listen and be patient, and you will know when you have learned enough about the objection to confidently resolve it.

4. **Always address ALL objections** before you ask for a commitment.

Chapter 16:
Closing the Sale or Gaining a Commitment

What You'll Learn in This Chapter:

1. Two questions you must be able to answer to know if you have made an effective close.

2. What you need to do before asking for a commitment.

The "close" or "commitment" is the big score, the Holy Grail, the crowning glory of the salesperson's profession. It really is the end goal of why we do what we do. There is a lot of satisfaction in the grand finale of convincing someone to accept your idea.

Whenever you see a group of salespeople talking, much of the time they are sharing stories about the close or commitment.

Evaluating Your Performance after Gaining a Commitment

At the end of a sales call, an easy way to evaluate your performance is by asking yourself two questions:

1. **What will the doctor do after my visit?**

   The hard part of this is being honest with yourself. At the beginning of your call, sit down and write out the following statement: "After I walk out the door, my physician is going to _____."

   This is the key to sales. Ultimately, you are trying to get your client to do something. Why else would you enter the office? At the end of your day, you must be able to honestly answer the question, "Will my client put any new patients on my drug?"

2. **Have I moved the client along in our treatment algorithm?**

   Is he going to use the product first line, versus using it when the standard first line product fails? Is he going to use the drug for something new? Maybe your client will refer his next problem patient to a certain specialist who you know favors your product.

Don't Rush the Commitment

The commitment is a logical conclusion to the discussion you have had in which you handled your client's objections. This step-by-step method is the logical framework of any type of conversation where ideas are transferred. If you try to gain a commitment to your ideas before the client is ready, you will set yourself back.

If you're not sure whether your client is ready, you can test this by using "pre-closing" statements to assess whether you have handled enough objections.

Some pre-closing questions might be:

- "How many patients in your practice would meet this type of criteria?"
- "Do you check with a patient what type of extended health plan they have?"

Over the years I have heard many discussions about the final part of any sales call. It used to be referred to as a close - you would close a sale. People were assessed as good closers or not good closers. Later it became known as "asking for the business."

The latest trendy term is "gaining a commitment." This comes from the distinction that you don't, in fact, want to *close* a sale; you want to *open* a new relationship.

All this is just fancy talk for something that revolves around one basic question: when you walk out the door, is that physician going to do as you hoped before you went in? If you were to ask the client if he would do what you wanted, would he say yes?

Really, the art and skill of gaining a commitment comes down to the first rule of sales: ask and you shall receive.

Key Strategies from This Chapter:

1. To determine if you have successfully gained a commitment, ask yourself, **"What will the client do after I leave the room?"** If they take the action you want, you have gained the commitment; if not, you may need to overcome some more objections.

2. **Be honest with yourself** when answering the above question! Be optimistic, of course, but not unrealistic. What will *really* happen when you walk out the door?

3. **Remember not to rush the commitment.** You cannot gain a commitment before overcoming all of your client's objections. It's better to spend more time on objections than to lose the commitment by presenting it too early in your interaction.

Chapter 17:
Post-Sale Follow Up

What You'll Learn in This Chapter:

1. Effective ways to ensure that the progress you made during the sales call is not lost when you walk out of the office.
2. How to leverage Rule Number Five (The best way to sell is to have someone else sell for you) after the sales call is done.
3. How to leverage Rule Number Seven (One sale can give you three others) and grow your sales exponentially.

At this point you may be able to see how all of the rules flow together. The sales call starts with the opening then leads to exploring the business, making a well-thought-out presentation, and working with the client through any objections or issues that they might have. Once the objections have all been addressed and the client is ready, we close the sale. But let's not stop here.

The post-sales follow up is extremely important and can make the difference between success and failure in sales. There is so much we can do to continue doing business with a happy client. Even if you gained a commitment once, you still need to plan how to do this again and again. You may have sold the client on the first visit, but people forget very easily.

Remember from the earlier sections how many times your clients have to be exposed to your product to remember it. There is a reason why you can finish this sentence: "Two all-beef patties ...." We have heard this so many times that it is ingrained in our minds.

On one occasion I was approached by a friend of mine who was selling a new bone density enhancer. She was new to the industry, and was hoping to gain more skills in selling pharmaceuticals. I started telling her what I knew of the business, and one of the first things I told her was that she would have to repeat the name of the drug to her client at least five times during the course of a meeting before her client would remember the name of it.

At that point, I realized that I had forgotten the name of the drug she was selling. She reminded me, and the conversation continued. After a little more discussion, I realized that I had forgotten again. She really did have to remind me five times during the conversation. Now, I often have a lot on my mind, but this was ridiculous. We had not even started discussing the dose, side effects, or precautions of the drug; all of which have been proven by research to help doctors feel comfortable enough to use a pharmaceutical product.

At the end of our conversation, my friend turned to me and asked in exasperation whether I was kidding with her just to prove a point. I was not kidding!

The best technique is to actually discuss this with the clients. The really good ones will acknowledge this with you and encourage you to help them remember. I usually call this a "habit breaking exercise". With this you get the client to agree that you will come in and visit repeatedly just to remind them of the product, the indication, and the dose. A good pharmaceutical marketer will give you a number of pieces that you can use when you come into the office to see the client.

The next stage comes when you have a client who has actually used the product and has some success with it. From here the game plan is to turn that client into someone who will tell others about the success. This is the heart of Rules Number Five and Seven. A really happy client should not only be speaking highly of your product to all their colleagues, but potentially telling you which colleagues you should be going to speak with.

Include this in many of your habit breaking exercises. See if they and another doctor will meet with you on your next visit to discuss disease management. This is an excellent way to get two clients together and one of the best uses of your lunch 'n' learn budget if you have one.

A journal club is another excellent way to engage the client with their peers. A journal club is a meeting with a number of clients to read and discuss a scientific journal. Think of it as a book club for doctors. When you are a part of a book club someone is elected to choose a book for everyone in the club to read. All the members of the club then take a couple of weeks or a month to read the book and then get together to discuss the book. Throw in a bottle of wine and some cheese and crackers, and this is a great way to spend the evening.

A journal club isn't very different. Usually one of the doctors picks a journal or two for the group to read, then once a month the group will get together and review the scientific journals. This is an excellent way for you to get the disease that your product treats into the discussion. Having a client already sold on the product can mean that a good scientific study will be placed into the review pool of a journal club.

Key Strategies from This Chapter:

1. **Maximize your post-sales strategy** to get your sales growing exponentially.

2. Encourage existing clients to lead you to more potential clients.

3. Get a client to agree to a "habit breaking" exercise early on to help you solidify the sale you have just won.

SECTION FOUR:
MOVING UP AND MOVING ON

Chapter 18:
Promotions, Raises, and Mentoring

What You'll Learn in This Chapter:

1. What to expect in terms of image and salary if you move from sales into marketing.

2. How to show your employer that you are interested in advancing.

3. How finding a mentor can help advance your career.

Marketing plays a huge role in the pharmaceutical industry, and moving from sales into marketing is seen as an advance in one's career.

Some people may only take positions in sales in order to advance into marketing. If marketing is your end goal, then getting a job within sales is an excellent first step.

Moving from Sales into Marketing

The role of marketing in the pharmaceutical industry can easily be explained by way of a military analogy. If we imagine a sales force as the front-line soldiers battling against an adversary or competitor, then the marketing department are the engineers designing the weapons that are used on the battlefield.

That being said, if your belief is that there is more money to be made in marketing, I have seen the opposite hold true in many cases. Usually in a good company that is committed to growth, the top-performing salespeople receive some of the highest salaries. Also, moving to marketing can decrease your overall earning power because in the office you lose your car allowance, which is a significant bonus on a salary.

Promotions and Raises

Promotions and raises go hand in hand because if you are successful at achieving one, then the other often follows. Selling skills will always help you open doors in this endeavor. Build your contacts within the company, find out what is needed in a particular position, then offer to fill it.

Remember Rule Number One: ask for the promotion and you will receive the promotion. Even when you suspect that you will not be given the position, asking about it sends a message to the executive that you are interested in advancing.

Finding a Mentor

It is a good idea to have a mentor who can guide you through your career. I have had quite a few mentors in my career, and will continue to seek more. These people are experienced in the industry and are quite approachable.

When I was getting started, my mentor was a specialist representative. I used to call him five times a day - sometimes after every sales call - just to bounce ideas off him and get answers to questions that would arise during my day-to-day business. It is amazing what can be thrown at you from pharmacists, nurses, and doctors during your day. I learned a lot from my mentor and gained a great friend.

We are still good friends to this day, and I still visit his house for barbeques when I am in his hometown. I have watched and learned a lot from his career as he has risen from being a sales rep to getting a position in marketing, eventually settling into a biotechnology firm. Our industry continues to grow, providing much work and room for growth and advancement for those seeking it.

Key Strategies from This Chapter:

1. Advancing from sales into marketing can be satisfying if that is your career goal, but be aware that **top-performing sales reps will generally earn more** through bonuses, a car allowance, and other perks.

2. **Ask for a promotion** and you are far more likely to get one. Remember the first rule of sales: "Ask and you shall receive!"

3. **Find a mentor** who is willing to help you learn the ropes when you are starting out. A good mentor can show you how to avoid "typical" mistakes and rise to the top far more quickly.

Chapter 19:
Work-Withs

What You'll Learn in This Chapter:

1. How to plan a successful "work-with" for you and your manager.

2. The best sales calls to make during a "work-with."

This chapter will be brief, and will provide you with an overview of what I believe is the best strategy for working with managers and senior executives.

First, let me remind you of my strong feeling that selling pharmaceuticals is an excellent job. One of the best aspects of this job is the freedom. Ninety percent of the time, you have no one with you; you are the master of your domain, and you can run your business as you wish.

But there is one aspect of the job that must be undertaken and performed well: working with upper management. This can include direct managers, product managers, medical managers, government or market access managers, directors, vice presidents, and even visiting international directors.

Survival Tips for Working with Upper Management

No doubt about it, working with upper management can be stressful at first, but it does get easier as you get better at and more comfortable in your job.

Here are three tips that will help you create a good impression with management and ensure that things go smoothly.

Tip #1: Use a "cheat sheet" to plan a successful day.

If a manager or company executive will be coming along on your sales calls, get prepared by writing out a cheat sheet for yourself. Plan your day!

Where are you going? What will you be doing? Who are you going to see? Ensure that you have the background history of the clients you go to see.

This step is the single most important step you can take to prepare for a successful day. It will help your work-with go smoothly and show that you are prepared for running your business.

Tip #2: "Stack the deck" with good calls.

Another key is to ensure that you have good calls all day.

Countless times, I have heard managers say, "I want to observe a typical work day." Don't fall into this trap. At the end of the day, I hear the same managers complaining about going to see a bunch of nurses and pharmacists all day, and not one prescriber.

It is important to see these people, but clients who prescribe should always be the main focus for a work-with. Stack the deck in your favor and make sure that a number of your calls are with clients who are easy to see and talk to.

Don't set up a day of hard-to-see clients until much later in your career. These days are frustrating, and your manager will share in your frustration. Ensure that you book calls with clients who actually prescribe your product.

Tip #3: Perception is reality.

Finally, make sure that you have all the tools you need during the day, including any detail pieces or marketing pieces you need, and that your car is clean. Perception is reality, and if your car looks totally disorganized the manager or executive may believe that you are as well.

Not that I agree - I have met many successful people with the most disorganized desks and offices. Still, keeping tidy creates a favourable impression.

Key Strategies from This Chapter:

1. **Use a "cheat sheet"** to plan a successful day and ensure that everything goes smoothly.

2. Don't make the mistake of planning a "typical" day. **Stack the deck in your favor** and make calls to your best prospects and clients.

3. **Make a good impression by cleaning your car**, dressing well, and making sure you have everything well organized before bringing management along for a work-with.

Chapter 20:
Nationals and Corporate Cycle Meetings...
or Just Out for Coffee

What You'll Learn in This Chapter:

1. What to expect at internal and inter-corporate meetings.

2. The fastest way to damage or ruin a career in sales.

Working for most corporations includes participating in many internal or inter-corporate meetings. These meetings are a great place to share information with colleagues, get updates on new strategies, and design new strategies for the future.

These meetings can be exhausting - you are working morning, noon, and night. Unless you are asleep or out for a walk there is very little downtime when you are at these meetings. They run for a week, and you are interacting with colleagues at every meal you have, as well as when you go out for drinks after a day's meeting.

Keep It Professional

The key to a successful meeting is to not get carried away. There is always a lot of alcohol around, and the mood is celebratory; you are being pumped up because of good results. I have seen many a career wrecked or damaged because a colleague had a few too many. Remember that this is business, and you are not out with your university buddies.

The same goes for every interaction you have, from your coffee shop meetings to your corporate meetings. Keep professional with every meeting within your organization. It is much harder than it seems.

Key Strategies from This Chapter:

1. Remember that a company meeting is not a visit with your university buddies. Watch your drinking and keep it professional.

2. **Any meeting, large or small, is business.** Stay professional in all your interactions.

SECTION FIVE:
LEGAL

Chapter 21:
Legal and Ethical Considerations

What You'll Learn in This Chapter:

1. How corporate scandals and mismanagement have changed the pharmaceutical industry.

2. Why "off-label" drug use continues.

Over the last 15 years the pharmaceutical industry has seen a major shift in thinking with respect to ethical and legal issues. The Enron and Worldcom scandals were the start of earthquakes that rocked the corporate world, and the tremors are still being felt today. Mismanagement of funds and corruption make headlines every day and are a huge focus in the media. As well as having to deal with this extra scrutiny of financial and transparency issues, the corporate world of pharmaceuticals has also had to deal with a massive shift in how drugs are reviewed and looked at by the regulatory branches of government.

The pharmaceutical industry has had its fair share of both scandal and change in the last few years. The amount of paperwork that is done now, compared to what was done 15 years ago, has gone up tenfold. For every report I used to write, I now write ten reports. This is in response to these scandals - now all of our work needs to be tracked and recorded to account for each dollar spent. This is all in the spirit of increased transparency.

The US introduced the "The Physician Payment Sunshine Act" in 2007, which requires that all pharmaceutical manufacturers collect, track, and disclose financial relationships that they have with physicians and teaching hospitals. All of this is meant to protect the patients from conflicts of interest that may occur due to financial relationships.

Increased paperwork, administration, and bureaucracy and decreased productivity are the by-products of some of these rules, but the upside is a much more accountable corporate world which is not at all a bad thing. Somewhere, a balance has to be found. The health care industry has always been in the spotlight; the ability to look after the sick is one of the pillars of any society.

Ethical Questions in the Pharmaceutical Industry

The pharmaceutical industry has never been without its ethical issues - in fact some of our biggest companies today got their meager starts from being involved in shady business. Merck Inc. was the first to market cocaine, which has amazing medicinal properties. (How does the slogan "Merck Fluffy White Flakes of Cocaine" grab you?) Bayer Pharmaceuticals was the first to add a couple carboxyl groups (C=O molecule) onto morphine and discover heroin, which from 1898 to 1910 was marketed as a non-addictive form of morphine. Research then was not what it is today.

There are many ways pharmaceutical companies are trying to address the concerns of legal and ethical decisions. An example would be the practice called "off-label" marketing - the promotion of a product without the proper label from the government.

The FDA (Food and Drug Administration) in the USA and Health Canada in Canada licence and authorize drugs for sale in their respective countries. Unless a company submits proper documentation to the appropriate agency, usually in the form of randomized, controlled Phase-Three studies, these groups will not authorize a drug for sale.

Off-label marketing has become a huge issue and has completely transformed the way pharmaceutical companies conduct business. One example is the charge that antidepressant manufacturers were promoting antidepressants for use in children. Later, data came out showing evidence that these products caused an increase in suicide among children. This and many other examples are why the pharmaceutical companies have completely changed these practices of late. Off-label use is a huge concern - according to some estimates, 31% to 93% of antipsychotic drugs are used off-label depending on the studies.

One reason for this is that products take years to go through trials to gain a label. This takes time and money to accomplish. Sometimes there would not be a market large enough to effectively run a trial, let alone make any profit from a small group of patients. Where does this leave the patient who could potentially need these drugs but is forced to wait until they are approved, *if* they are approved? The answers to questions like these are seldom simple.

To understand this, a person just has to have someone close to them die of cancer after going through all of the options available through the usual channels. I had one of my best friends die of a brain tumour after going through all of the "approved" uses. In the end he was desperate for anything to try to fight the disease. It is sad because there are a number of people that will sell these desperate people anything in order to help cure them.

Off-label use is a major issue in the pharmaceutical industry, as many companies have faced very stiff fines over this type of promotion. These days most, if not all, companies have entire divisions of compliance officers whose main job is to ensure that these problems do not ever occur and that the company cannot be sued for selling in this way. In many ways the compliance and legal departments are a large part of running the company.

Because pharmaceuticals are such an integral part of healthcare, we can expect that ethical scrutiny will do nothing but increase as time goes on. Our population is aging and the government is more and more involved in helping to ensure that people have access to proper healthcare. You will need to be familiar with the issues that have faced the industry in the past as well as those that present in the future.

Key Strategies from This Chapter:

1. Be aware that the pharmaceutical industry is affected by other industries. Public perception of corporate scandals and mismanagement has resulted in more scrutiny – and more paperwork – for our industry.

2. Know that off-label drug use is a complex issue. **As much as 50% to 80% of all drugs are used off-label**, often by physicians who feel that they cannot wait for regulatory bodies to approve these drugs.

Conclusion

My goal in writing this book has been to share with you the hard-won secrets I have learned about rising up through the pharmaceutical industry. I have taken you from finding contacts within the industry, to maximizing the value of these contacts, to increasing your level of experience and value within the profession. If you use these techniques, you will have the potential to earn a small fortune and find success within a rewarding career.

We have explored issues such as getting hired, going through company training, and surviving a work-with - all things that you will deal with on a regular basis. After reading this book, you will be able to speak intelligently and from a well-informed standpoint while interviewing and meeting with those already employed in the industry.

Once you have successfully gained employment within the industry you will continue to gain more in-depth knowledge of the day-to-day workings of this business, all of which should drastically decrease the steepness of the learning curve.

The key to success in this industry lies in recognizing one core belief: pharmaceuticals must be sold.

Selling is a craft that has existed for many thousands of years. Everything must be sold, and pharmaceuticals are no different. Many chapters in this book share tips and strategies on selling, but these are only a brief outline to help you obtain access to the industry. Perseverance is a key factor, because over the years many doors will be shut in your face. For a salesperson, this is part of life.

Continue to enhance your selling skills. They are transferable not only to other industries and areas of interest, but to many other aspects of life as well. Remember the seven rules of sales:

Rule #1: Ask and you shall receive.

Rule #2: Two ears, one mouth.

Rule #3: Whoever speaks first loses.

Rule #4: The 80/20 rule.

Rule #5: The best way to sell is having someone sell for you.

Rule #6: Do not preach in the desert.

Rule #7: One sale gives you three others.

All of these rules apply to the process I outlined in the sales section. From the initial greeting to arranging the financing to be made in the closing of the sale, the rules apply. The sooner you are able to master your selling skills, the more successful you will become at any job you do. And of course, promotions and raises will follow.

To conclude, I will cite Rule Number Two: "Two Ears, One Mouth." Please don't hesitate to contact me at **scottellerbeck1@gmail.com** if you have any comments or questions. I would love to hear your feedback.

Made in the USA
Middletown, DE
23 September 2021